50 + Retirement Roadmap

A Practical Step-by-Step Guide To Secure your Pension

Cassandra E. Morrison

COPYRIGHT © 2023 BY Cassandra E. Morrison

TABLE OF CONTENT

INTRODUCTION

Susan found herself at a crossroads in the latter stages of her profession, which would profoundly alter the course of her life.

It was a crisp autumn morning when she received the unexpected news of an early retirement offer from the employer she had committed decades to.

As she struggled with the unanticipated change in her life's course, shock and confusion washed over her like a tidal wave.

Retirement? Was she ready for this? Doubt and worry filled her head, and the formerly distant concept of retiring suddenly loomed before her like an impassable mountain.

The security of the usual routine at work was slipping away, leaving Susan with a profound feeling of inner instability and a burning yearning for change.

As she glanced out the window, watching the leaves fall slowly to the earth, a combination of emotions rushed through her.

She had spent years putting her heart and soul into her job, finding meaning and joy in the difficulties it presented.

Now, the notion of retirement felt like a huge vacuum, devoid of purpose and significance.

Her heart sank at the thought of leaving behind the bonds of friendship of her coworkers and the sense of pride that came with each successful assignment.

Amidst the jumble of emotions, Susan's head whirled with numerous questions. Would she have enough money to sustain her present lifestyle?

What would her days be like without the framework of work?

And maybe most significantly, who would she be if not for the title she had long kept with pride?

Perhaps you, too, find yourself standing in Susan's shoes, considering the undiscovered seas of retirement planning.

The weight of uncertainty and the dread of the unknown can feel overpowering, leaving you wondering if you have what it takes to traverse this new chapter of life.

But hear this: you are not alone on this path.

If you're reading this, it means that, like Susan, you're looking for suggestions, encouragement, and a sense of control over how to create the retirement you deserve.

This isn't simply another boring retirement book chock full of numbers and cold facts. It serves as a lifeline, a ray of hope, and a road plan for finding your sense of direction to retirement free of worries .

Within the pages of this book, is a compassionate guide that truly resonates with your worries, hopes, and goals. It's not just about money; it's about reclaiming your life and making the most of your golden years.

But it doesn't stop there! This book is not just about inspiration; it's about action. It's a practical toolbox filled with step-by-step strategies to empower you to take control of your retirement destiny.

You'll learn how to align your retirement goals with your core values, craft a robust financial plan that brings you peace of mind, and tackle every challenge with confidence.

Each chapter is packed with concrete tasks, providing you with the knowledge and tools to make informed decisions for your future.

Whether it's maximizing your retirement accounts, diversifying your assets, developing a flexible budget, or defining your retirement vision, this book leaves no stone unturned in your journey towards a fulfilling retirement.

So, dear friend, take my hand, and let's embark on this transformative trip together. With every turn of the page, you'll find not only inspiration but tangible strategies that will propel you towards a satisfying and secure retirement.

Now is the time to take action. The power to reshape your future lies within your grasp.

You have the power to redefine retirement on your terms as you go through it. Trust yourself, adopt this strategy, and let the retirement reinvention journey begin.

The world is ready for you to embrace your dream future beyond 50 with open arms.

Are you ready to claim the extraordinary retirement you deserve? Then let's get started! The journey awaits, and your best days are yet to come.

CHAPTER 1

The Road to a Secure Retirement

Retirement is a significant life event that requires careful preparation. It's a time when you can finally step back from the daily grind and focus on the things that truly matter to you.

However, without proper planning, retirement can be riddled with financial stress and uncertainty.
If you haven't started planning for retirement, don't worry – now is the perfect time to begin!

Procrastination can be tempting, but remember that the sooner you start, the more time you have to build your nest egg and achieve your desired retirement lifestyle.

Even if you're approaching retirement age, it's not too late to make a positive impact on your future.

So, if you are ready to seize control of your financial future and embark on the path towards a stress-free retirement? Let's get started!

The Importance of Retirement Planning

Retirement planning is more than just crunching numbers; it's like charting a course for your future happiness and security.

Think of it as a life strategy that can have a profound impact on your well-being as you move through your career journey.

When you finally reach retirement, it's like crossing a major milestone – a time to reap the rewards of all your hard work and bask in the joy of your well-earned savings.

The importance of retirement planning cannot be emphasized enough. It forms the bedrock of a fulfilling life after you bid farewell to the workforce.

It's like drawing a picture of the lifestyle you've always dreamed of during your golden years and then taking those necessary steps to turn that dream into a beautiful reality.

Let take a look at some few

1. **Future Happiness and Security:** Retirement planning is like charting a course for your future happiness and security. It's a

life strategy that profoundly impacts your well-being as you progress through your career journey.

2. **Celebrating Milestones:** When retirement finally arrives, it's like crossing a major milestone where you can reap the rewards of your hard work and bask in the joy of your well-earned savings.

3. **Foundation for Fulfillment:** Retirement planning forms the bedrock of a fulfilling life after bidding farewell to the workforce. It allows you to draw a vivid picture of your desired lifestyle during your golden years and take steps to turn that dream into a beautiful reality.

4. **Control Over Financial Destiny:** With a well-thought-out retirement plan, you gain a sense of control over your financial destiny. Aligning your savings, investments, and expenses brings a feeling of financial security and peace of mind.

5. **Safety Net for Surprises:** Life is full of surprises, but retirement planning acts as a safety net, helping you navigate unforeseen challenges without compromising your envisioned lifestyle or financial well-being.

6. **Excitement for the Future**: As retirement age approaches, planning becomes even more significant – it's like preparing for a

thrilling adventure. A well-prepared retirement journey transforms anxiety into anticipation for this exciting new phase of life.

7. **Exploring Dreams and Passions**: Retirement planning opens doors to a world of possibilities. It's an opportunity to uncover a treasure trove of experiences waiting to be enjoyed, from pursuing new interests to cherishing moments with loved ones.

8. **Personalized Path:** Each retirement journey is unique – creating a personalized map that suits your preferences, circumstances, and dreams. Thoughtful consideration and professional advice shape the decisions that will define your future.

9. **Seizing the Moment:** This is your time, your life, and your future. Through thoughtful and heartfelt retirement planning, you can truly make it yours – embracing the possibilities and making the most of this remarkable journey

So,this is your time, your life, and your future – make it truly yours through thoughtful and heartfelt retirement planning.

Dispelling Myths and Misconceptions of Retirement Planning

Let's shed some light on those retirement planning myths that seem to float around everywhere. We're here to set the record straight!

Myth 1: "I'm Too Old to Start Planning.

Hold on just a minute! It's understandable to feel like time may be slipping away, but age is no barrier when it comes to retirement planning.

It's never too late to set sail towards a brighter financial future. No matter where you are in life, every step counts! Whether you're in your 50s, 60s, or beyond, proactive planning can make a significant difference in your retirement readiness.

By starting now, you're taking the helm of your financial ship and steering it towards a secure and enjoyable retirement.

Myth 2: "I Can Rely Solely on Social Security.

Social Security is like a gentle breeze helping your ship along, providing a safety net for your retirement.

However, relying solely on Social Security may not be enough to ensure smooth sailing throughout your golden years.

Social Security benefits are designed to replace only a portion of your pre-retirement income, and for many individuals, they may not cover all of their post-retirement expenses.

That's why it's crucial to supplement your Social Security benefits with other income sources.

Creating a diverse portfolio of income streams, including pensions, retirement accounts, and personal investments, will strengthen your financial sails and keep your journey steady and strong.

Myth 3: "I Don't Need to Worry About Healthcare Costs.

Healthcare costs are indeed a real concern, mate. As you set sail on your retirement voyage, you'll want to ensure you're well-prepared to navigate potential medical expenses.

Healthcare costs can be significant, and without proper planning, they may put a strain on your finances.

It's essential to explore options for healthcare coverage, such as Medicare and supplemental insurance, to help you weather any unforeseen medical storms.

Moreover, adopting a healthy lifestyle now can help keep you in good shape for the long voyage ahead, potentially reducing medical expenses down the line.

Fear 1: "What If I Outlive My Savings?

That's a common worry, but there are ways to set a course to avoid this situation. One of the key factors in retirement planning is estimating your life expectancy and ensuring that your savings will last throughout your entire journey.

By crafting a well-thought-out retirement plan that factors in various scenarios, you can find peace of mind knowing that you've taken steps to protect yourself against outliving your resources.

Consider diversifying your investments, exploring options like annuities, and making strategic decisions about when to claim Social Security benefits.

These actions will help you keep your treasure chest full and sail smoothly through your golden years.

Fear 2: "I'm Afraid of Making the Wrong Choices.

Yes, making financial decisions can feel like charting uncharted waters. The thought of handling your hard-earned money wisely can be overwhelming.

But don't fret; you don't have to sail solo! Seeking advice can guide you towards the best route for your retirement goals. Just like you've taken the first step with this book, rest assured that you are on the right path.

Fear 3: "I'll Never Achieve My Retirement Goals.

Let's cast that fear aside. It's entirely normal to worry about whether you'll have enough resources to achieve your retirement dreams.

But remember, with proper planning and determination, you can set sail towards your goals. Start by defining clear and realistic retirement objectives.

Break them down into manageable steps, and celebrate each milestone along the way. Consider increasing your retirement contributions, finding ways to reduce expenses, and exploring additional income streams to bolster your retirement funds.

Not to worry, In the following chapters, we'll break down these strategies in detail and provide expert guidance on how to achieve them step by step accompanied with practical exercises.

With each small victory, your confidence will grow, and you'll be well on your way to reaching your retirement dreams.

Fear 4: "I'm Nervous About Market Volatility.

The ever-changing tides of the financial markets can be intimidating. You might worry about your investments weathering storms and market downturns.

While market fluctuations are inevitable, a diversified investment strategy can help you navigate these waters with more confidence.

Rest assured, we've taken the time to address this comprehensively in one of our chapters. Armed with knowledge and guided by a strategic plan, you can confidently face market fluctuations and stay on track to achieve your financial goals.

Remember, it's crucial to stay focused on your long-term goals and avoid making rash decisions based on short-term market movements.

Understanding the Need for Financial Security

Let's talk about something essential as we prepare for retirement: financial security. It's like building a strong foundation to support the life you want to lead during this exciting phase of life.

The Importance of Achieving Financial Security

Imagine a retirement where you have the financial freedom to pursue your passions and enjoy life to the fullest.

Financial security offers just that—the peace of mind that comes with knowing you have enough resources to cover your expenses and live comfortably without constant worry about money.

Financial security during retirement means you can confidently face whatever comes your way. It's like having a safety net to protect you from unexpected challenges, giving you the ability to weather storms and embrace life with confidence.

You'll have the flexibility to make choices that align with your values and aspirations, whether it's traveling, spending time with loved ones, or pursuing new hobbies.

But let's be real: achieving financial security in retirement requires thoughtful planning and preparation. It's not something that happens overnight; it's a journey that requires time, effort, and dedication.

However, with the strategies discussed in this book, you can set yourself up for a secure and fulfilling retirement.

Potential Challenges and Risks Without Proper Planning

As we set the course for retirement, it's crucial to be aware of potential challenges and risks that might arise if we don't plan wisely.

Let's take a closer look at some of these challenges:

Rising Life Expectancy: People are living longer, which is undoubtedly a reason to celebrate! However, a longer life also means a longer retirement period to plan for. It's essential to ensure that your financial resources can sustain you throughout those extra years, so you can enjoy life to the fullest.

Inflation: The cost of living tends to increase over time due to inflation. What seems like a comfortable amount of money today may not stretch as far in the future. To combat the effects of inflation, it's essential to have investments that can potentially outpace rising costs and protect the purchasing power of your savings.

Healthcare Costs: As we age, the likelihood of facing health-related expenses increases. Healthcare costs can be a significant factor in retirement planning, and without proper preparation, they can become a financial burden. Exploring options like Medicare and insurance can provide added peace of mind to handle potential health challenges.

Market Volatility: Financial markets can be unpredictable, and market fluctuations can impact the value of your investments. Without a well-diversified portfolio and a solid investment strategy, you might find yourself navigating choppy waters.

Social Security Uncertainties: While Social Security benefits are a valuable component of retirement income, there may be uncertainties and potential changes to the system.

To ensure a smoother journey, it's essential to view Social Security benefits as one piece of your retirement puzzle and explore other income sources to bolster your financial security.one of the chapters extensively discussed this.

CHAPTER 2

Set Retirement Goals

In this chapter, we'll explore the profound impact of defining your retirement vision, where every stroke of your imagination paints a vivid picture of your ideal retirement lifestyle.

From the places you wish to explore to the activities that bring you joy, we'll uncover the very essence of what makes your heart sing during this well-earned chapter of life.

Whether you dream of cultural exploration, a cozy retreat by the shore, or simply cherishing moments with loved ones, your retirement goals will lay the foundation for an extraordinary and purposeful retirement.

Step 1: Determine Your Ideal Retirement Age and Reasons

Congratulations on taking the first step towards a brighter and more fulfilling future! Deciding when you want to retire is a momentous decision, and it's essential to make this choice with thoughtful consideration and confidence.

In this step, we'll explore how to determine your ideal retirement age and take a look into the reasons that will shape this pivotal milestone in your life.

Reflect on Work-Life balance.

Your ideal retirement age is also closely tied to your work-life balance. Consider how much time you want to spend on your career versus enjoying the fruits of your labor in retirement.

Are you eager to retire early and pursue other passions, or do you find fulfillment in continuing to work?

For instance, if you cherish your current job and find it personally rewarding, you might opt for a phased retirement approach. This way, you can gradually reduce your work hours while still being engaged in your profession.

Align with Life Milestones

Life is full of milestones, and your ideal retirement age may align with significant events in your life. Reflect on your family's needs and commitments, such as supporting children through college or caring for elderly parents.

For example, if your youngest child is entering college in five years, you might plan your retirement age to coincide with their graduation. This way, you can provide support during their educational journey while also transitioning smoothly into the next phase of your life.

Remember that choosing your retirement age is a personal decision, and there's no one-size-fits-all answer. Your ideal retirement age should reflect your dreams, aspirations, and readiness to embrace the golden years with joy and fulfillment.

Step 2: Consider Your Desired Retirement Lifestyle

As you journey towards retirement, envisioning your desired lifestyle is a crucial step in creating a roadmap for your golden years.

Retirement is not merely a destination; it's an opportunity to craft a life that aligns with your passions, values, and aspirations.

In this section, we'll explore the process of defining your retirement lifestyle, including where you want to live and the activities that will bring you joy and fulfillment.

Reflect on Your Dreams and aspirations.

Take a moment to reflect on what brings you the most joy and satisfaction. Consider the following questions:

Where do you envision yourself living during retirement? Is it in your current home, downsizing to a cozy apartment, or perhaps moving closer to your loved ones?

What activities or hobbies have always intrigued you but were put on hold due to work commitments? How would you like to incorporate them into your retirement lifestyle?

Are there any new skills you'd like to learn or adventures you'd love to embark on? Imagine the sense of accomplishment and excitement that awaits you in your golden years.

For example, if you've always dreamed of living near the ocean and feeling the sand between your toes, retiring to a coastal town might be the perfect choice for you. Imagine waking up to the sound of seagulls and taking daily strolls along the beach, immersing yourself in the serenity of the waves.

This vision can inspire you to plan your retirement with a focus on making this dream a reality.

Consider Your Preferred Living environment.

Your living environment plays a significant role in shaping your retirement experience. Think about the type of community and climate that resonate with your lifestyle preferences.

Are you drawn to the bustling energy of city life or the tranquility of a rural setting?

Do you prefer a close-knit community with plenty of social activities or a more private and secluded retreat?

What climate best suits your preferences and health needs? Some individuals enjoy the changing seasons, while others prefer a milder and sunnier climate.

For instance, if you're passionate about nature and enjoy outdoor activities like hiking, biking, and gardening, retiring to a countryside retreat with lush greenery and scenic landscapes might be your ideal choice.

Being close to nature can provide endless opportunities for relaxation and rejuvenation.

Explore Activities that Bring fulfillment.

Retirement is an opportunity to explore activities that ignite your passion and sense of purpose. Consider the following aspects:

Are you interested in engaging in volunteer work and giving back to the community?

Would you like to join clubs or organizations that share your interests, providing opportunities to connect with like-minded individuals?

What types of physical activities or exercises do you enjoy, and how can you incorporate them into your daily routine to stay active and healthy?

For example, suppose you've always had a passion for supporting a cause close to your heart, such as animal welfare.

In that case, you might want to dedicate part of your retirement to volunteering at a local animal shelter or wildlife conservation organization. This allows you to make a meaningful impact while finding fulfillment in your post-career years.

Consider Proximity to Family and friends.

Your relationships with family and friends are vital to your overall well-being and happiness. Consider how your retirement lifestyle aligns with maintaining strong connections with your loved ones.

Do you want to live near your adult children and grandchildren to be an active part of their lives?

How can you foster a sense of community and camaraderie among your circle of friends during retirement?

For instance, if being close to family is a priority, you might explore retirement communities or neighborhoods that are conveniently located near your loved ones. This way, you can share cherished moments and create lasting memories with your family, enriching your retirement experience.

Financial Considerations

As you envision your retirement lifestyle, it's crucial to align your dreams with your financial capabilities. Assess the financial requirements of your desired lifestyle, including housing costs, travel expenses, and any other significant activities you plan to pursue.

For example, suppose your retirement vision includes traveling to different countries and exploring new cultures. In that case, you'll need to budget for travel expenses, accommodations, and any experiences you wish to indulge in during your journeys.

Embrace Flexibility and adaptability.

Retirement is a dynamic phase of life, and your desires and interests may evolve over time. Embrace the flexibility to adapt your retirement lifestyle as needed to accommodate changes and new opportunities that arise.

For example, as your family dynamics change or new hobbies capture your interest, be open to adjusting your retirement plans accordingly. Embracing flexibility allows you to flow with life's transitions and make the most of each moment.

Remember, your retirement lifestyle is uniquely yours, and there's no right or wrong way to design it.

Embrace the freedom to create a retirement that reflects your values, aspirations, and passions.

Step 3: Decide How Many Years Post-Retirement You Want to Plan for

Planning for your retirement is not just about preparing for the day you officially retire; it's about envisioning the years that follow and making provisions for the future.

As you embark on this step, it's essential to consider how many years post-retirement you want to plan for, taking into account potential life expectancy and unforeseen circumstances.

This forward-thinking approach will empower you to create a robust retirement plan that ensures financial security throughout your golden years.

Assess Your Life expectancy.

Estimating your life expectancy is a crucial element of retirement planning. While none of us can predict the future with certainty, understanding average life expectancies can provide valuable insights.

Factors such as genetics, lifestyle choices, and overall health influence life expectancy.

For example, let's say you're currently 55 years old and in good health. Based on your family's history and your healthy lifestyle, you may reasonably expect to live well into your 80s or even 90s.

This means planning for a retirement period of 30 years or more.

Consider Potential Unforeseen circumstances.

Life is unpredictable, and it's essential to factor in unforeseen circumstances when planning for your retirement years.

These circumstances may include health issues, unforeseen expenses, changes in family dynamics, or economic fluctuations. While it's impossible to prepare for every eventuality, having contingency plans can provide a safety net.

For example, suppose you plan to retire at 65 and envision a fulfilling retirement filled with travel and leisure activities. However, a few years into retirement, you face unexpected medical expenses due to a health condition.

Having a financial cushion or insurance coverage in place can help alleviate the financial strain and ensure you can continue to enjoy your retirement lifestyle.

Account for Potential Changes in Lifestyle

As you plan for the years post-retirement, keep in mind that your lifestyle preferences may evolve over time.

While you may have specific aspirations in mind now, your interests and priorities could shift as you enter different phases of retirement.

For example, in the early years of retirement, you may be more focused on travel and exploration. As you age, you might prefer a more relaxed and locally oriented lifestyle, engaging in activities that bring you joy and fulfillment within your community.

Being open to adjusting your retirement plans ensures that your financial strategy remains adaptable and flexible.

Revisit and Adjust Your Plan regularly.

Retirement planning is not a one-time exercise; it's an ongoing process. As you move through retirement, periodically revisit and reassess your financial plan.

Changes in market conditions, lifestyle choices, and family dynamics may necessitate adjustments to your strategy.

Practical Exercise: Retirement Vision Board

Congratulations on reaching this exciting stage of your retirement planning journey! Creating a retirement vision board is a powerful and creative way to bring your retirement dreams to life.

This hands-on exercise will help you gain clarity, motivation, and inspiration as you envision the retirement you've always imagined.

The process of crafting your retirement vision board will tap into your deepest aspirations, allowing you to visualize and manifest the retirement lifestyle you desire.

Step 1: Gather Your Materials

To get started, gather the materials you'll need to create your retirement vision board. Here's what you'll need:

- A large poster board or corkboard: Choose a size that gives you ample space to arrange your visual elements.
- Magazines, newspapers, or printed images: Look for images that represent your retirement goals, such as travel destinations, hobbies, activities, and personal interests.

Focus on pictures that resonate with you and evoke positive emotions.

- Scissors and glue sticks: These will be your trusty tools for cutting out images and adhering them to your vision board.
- Colored markers, pens, or stickers: Use these to add inspiring words, quotes, or symbols that reinforce your retirement vision.

Step 2: Reflect on Your Retirement Goals

Before you start creating your retirement vision board, take some time to reflect on your retirement goals. Consider the following questions:

- What activities or hobbies do you want to pursue during retirement?
- Where do you envision spending your time? Are there specific travel destinations you want to explore?
- How do you envision your ideal living situation during retirement?
- What relationships do you want to nurture and cultivate during this phase of life?
- How do you envision maintaining your health and well-being in retirement?
- What financial milestones do you want to achieve to support your retirement goals?

Step 3: Bring Your Retirement Vision to Life

Now that you've reflected on your retirement goals, it's time to create your retirement vision board.

Begin by cutting out images and words from magazines or printing them from online sources that align with your retirement aspirations.

Arrange them on the board in a way that feels visually appealing and meaningful to you.

For example, if one of your retirement goals is to travel and explore new places, find images of your dream destinations.

If you want to spend more time with family and friends, include pictures that represent cherished moments with loved ones. If you aspire to live in a serene beachside community, find images that evoke the tranquility of coastal living.

As you create your vision board, remember that there are no right or wrong choices—this is a personal and expressive process meant to capture your unique vision of retirement. Trust your instincts and choose images and words that deeply resonate with your heart.

Step 4: Reflect and Revisit

Your retirement vision board is not just a one-time project; it's a dynamic and evolving representation of your aspirations.

Place your vision board in a prominent location where you'll see it daily, such as your bedroom, office, or meditation space.

Take a few moments each day to reflect on the images and words on your board, allowing them to inspire and motivate you on your retirement planning journey.

As you progress through your retirement planning, feel free to add new elements to your vision board or adjust it based on evolving goals and aspirations.

Your retirement vision board is a living reminder of the life you are creating for yourself, and it will serve as a powerful source of inspiration and motivation as you work towards your retirement dreams.

CHAPTER 3

Take Stock of Your Current Financial situation.

Identifying your assets and investments is a crucial step in our journey towards a secure retirement.

Think of it as navigating the intricate map of your financial terrain, uncovering the treasures you've accumulated over the years.

In this chapter, we'll explore the process of assessing your financial resources, ensuring that no valuable gem goes unnoticed.

Start with a Comprehensive List:

To begin, gather all your financial documents and records in one place. Create a comprehensive list that includes your assets, investments, savings, and any other financial holdings.

This list serves as a treasure map, guiding you through your financial landscape.

Assets: Your assets encompass everything you own that has value. Include your primary residence, vacation homes, vehicles, valuable jewelry, and any other tangible possessions.

Remember, even those family heirlooms may contribute to your overall financial picture.

Example: Your primary residence, a cozy house nestled by the waterfront, is a valuable asset that you've cherished for decades. Its current market value holds immense potential for your retirement plans.

Investments: These may include stocks, bonds, mutual funds, certificates of deposit (CDs), and real estate properties. Each investment plays a unique role in building your financial strength.

Example: Over the years, you've wisely invested in a diversified portfolio of stocks and bonds, carefully balancing risk and return. These investments have grown steadily, laying the foundation for your future financial security.

Savings: This Include all types of savings, such as emergency funds, cash reserves, and other liquid assets.

Retirement Accounts: This Include all your Individual Retirement Accounts (IRAs), 401(k)s, 403(b)s, or any other employer-sponsored retirement plans.

Example: Your 401(k) account, diligently contributed to over the years, will play a significant role in financing your retirement adventures.

Assess the Value of Each Asset:

Once you've assembled your treasure list, it's time to determine the current value of each asset. Real estate properties and valuable possessions may require professional appraisals, while financial accounts can be easily accessed online or through statements.

Example: You decide to have your primary residence appraised to get an accurate estimate of its current market value. Additionally, you review your investment account statements to gauge the current worth of your diversified portfolio.

Consider Tax Implications:

As you navigate your financial terrain, keep a keen eye on tax implications. Some assets may carry tax advantages, while others could have tax consequences during withdrawal or sale.

Example: You're aware that your retirement accounts, such as IRAs and 401(k)s, may have tax advantages during the accumulation phase.

However, distributions during retirement may be subject to income taxes.

Evaluate Liabilities

While identifying your assets, don't forget to assess your liabilities, such as mortgages, loans, and outstanding debts. Subtract your liabilities from your assets to determine your net worth, a crucial indicator of your financial strength.

Example: After calculating your total liabilities, including a remaining mortgage and a small car loan, you find that your net worth is significantly positive, bringing a sense of financial security.

By meticulously identifying your assets and investments, you're better equipped to make informed decisions about your retirement goals.

This step is a cornerstone of effective retirement planning, ensuring that your financial resources align with your envisioned retirement lifestyle.

With your financial landscape thoroughly explored, we'll continue our voyage towards building a comprehensive retirement plan that will lead you to the future you desire.

Make a Comprehensive List of Liabilities:

To begin, compile a comprehensive list of all your liabilities, including debts and outstanding obligations. This list will serve as a detailed map of your financial obligations, guiding us through potential challenges.

Debts: List all your debts, such as credit card balances, personal loans, student loans, and any other outstanding loans. Include the total amount owed, minimum monthly payments, and interest rates.

Example: Your credit card debt, which you've been working diligently to pay off, is part of your overall liabilities. Its current balance and interest rate are important considerations in your financial analysis.

Mortgages: If you have a mortgage on your primary residence or any other properties, include the remaining balance, interest rate, and monthly payments.

Example: Your mortgage on the primary residence you cherish is an essential liability that impacts your financial planning.

Other Obligations: Don't forget to include any other financial obligations, such as car loans, medical bills, or other outstanding debts.

Calculate the Total Liabilities:

After creating a comprehensive list, calculate the total amount of your liabilities. This sum represents the combined burden of your debts and obligations.

Example: You sum up all your debts, mortgages, and other obligations to determine your total liabilities.

Compare Liabilities to Assets:

Now, it's time to compare your total liabilities to the value of your assets. This comparison helps us understand your net worth and how your assets stack up against your financial obligations.

Example: You calculate your net worth by subtracting your total liabilities from the total value of your assets. A positive net worth indicates that your assets outweigh your liabilities, while a negative net worth may signal areas of concern.

Assess Debt Repayment Strategies:

If you find that your liabilities outweigh your assets or if you have substantial debt, it's essential to develop a debt repayment strategy. Focus on paying down high-interest debts first to reduce overall interest costs.

Example: You decide to prioritize paying off your credit card debt with the highest interest rate, as it will have the most significant impact on reducing your overall debt burden.

Consider Long-Term Obligations:

Be mindful of any long-term obligations, such as future college tuition for children or potential healthcare expenses. These commitments may impact your financial planning during retirement.

Example: You anticipate future college tuition expenses for your grandchildren and begin to explore options for contributing to their education funds.

Analyzing your liabilities is a fundamental step in understanding your financial landscape. By comprehensively assessing your debts and obligations, you're better equipped to make informed decisions about your retirement goals.

Assessing Your Retirement Preparedness: Reviewing Your Current Allocations

Now, let's move on to an important task of checking if you already have funds allocated to retirement planning.

Gather Information on Existing Retirement Accounts:

Begin by gathering all the necessary information about your existing retirement accounts. These may include 401(k)s, IRAs (Individual Retirement Accounts), pension plans, or any other employer-sponsored retirement plans.

Example: You have a 401(k) account from your previous job and an IRA that you've been contributing to regularly.

Review Contributions and Investment Performance:

Once you have the details of your retirement accounts, review your contribution history and the performance of your investments.

Understanding your past contributions and the growth of your investments will provide valuable insights into the progress you've made so far.

Assess Fees and Expenses:

As you review your retirement accounts, also assess any fees and expenses associated with them. High fees can significantly impact your overall returns, so it's essential to be aware of these costs.

Example: You discover that your 401(k) has higher administrative fees compared to your low-cost IRA. You may consider consolidating your retirement accounts to reduce fees and simplify management.

Consider Rollover Options:

If you have retirement accounts from previous employers, consider the option of rolling them over into an IRA or your current employer's retirement plan. Rollovers can provide more control and flexibility over your investments.

Evaluate Overall Retirement Readiness

After conducting a thorough review of your existing retirement accounts, step back and evaluate your overall retirement readiness. Take into account any additional savings or investments outside of retirement accounts that can contribute to your retirement goals.

Example: Considering your existing retirement accounts and other investments, you feel confident about your progress towards a secure retirement but want to explore further options for continued growth.

Checking your existing retirement accounts provides a solid starting point for planning your retirement. It allows you to leverage what you already have and build upon it strategically.

Practical Exercise: Personal Net Worth Statement

It's time to roll up your sleeves and embark on a practical and insightful exercise: creating your very own net worth statement.

This exercise will serve as a powerful tool to help you gauge your current financial standing and pave the way for a successful retirement plan.

Just like a skilled cartographer maps out uncharted territories, you'll be mapping your financial landscape by listing all your assets and liabilities.

Step 1: Gather Your Financial Information

To begin, gather all your financial documents and information. This includes statements for your bank accounts, investment accounts, retirement accounts, properties, vehicles, and any other significant assets you own.

Additionally, collect records of your outstanding debts, loans, mortgages, and credit card balances.

Step 2: List Your Assets

Now, let's take stock of your assets. On a sheet of paper or a digital spreadsheet, create two columns: one for assets and another for their corresponding values. Start listing all your assets in the designated column. This may include:

Cash: The money you have in your savings and checking accounts

Investments: Stocks, bonds, mutual funds, and any other investment holdings

Retirement Accounts: Your 401(k), IRA, or any other retirement savings

Real Estate: The value of your primary residence, vacation homes, or investment properties

Vehicles: The estimated value of your cars, boats, or other vehicles

Personal Property: Valuable items like jewelry, artwork, or collectibles

Business Interests: If you own a business, estimate its value.

For each asset, be realistic and use current market values. While it's essential to be thorough, don't worry about being overly precise; approximate values are sufficient for this exercise.

Step 3: Account for Your Liabilities

Now, let's tackle your liabilities—the debts and financial obligations you owe. Create another two-column list for liabilities and their corresponding amounts. Include items such as:

Mortgages: The outstanding balances on your home or any other properties you own

Loans: Personal loans, auto loans, student loans, or any other outstanding debts

Credit Card Balances: The amounts you owe on your credit cards

Remember to include all your liabilities, no matter how small. This exercise aims to provide a comprehensive picture of your financial situation.

Step 4: Calculate Your Net Worth

With your assets and liabilities listed, it's time to calculate your net worth. To do this, subtract the total value of your liabilities from the total value of your assets. The result is your net worth, a crucial indicator of your current financial health.

Step 5: Evaluate Your Financial Progress

Congratulations! You now have a personalized net worth statement that lays out your financial landscape. As you move forward with your retirement planning, regularly update this statement to track your progress.

Comparing your net worth over time will help you evaluate the effectiveness of your financial decisions and the impact of your retirement strategy.

Remember, this exercise isn't just about the numbers; it's about gaining a deeper understanding of your financial position and setting the course for a secure and prosperous retirement.

CHAPTER 4

Estimating Retirement Expenses

Now that you've defined your retirement vision and set clear goals, it's time to transform those dreams into actionable plans.

In this chapter, we'll guide you through the process of calculating and planning your monthly retirement contributions.

Just like a skilled navigator adjusts the sails to follow the chosen course, you'll strategically set aside funds to build your nest egg and sail towards the retirement of your dreams.

By taking these well-informed steps, you'll be on track to secure a rewarding and worry-free retirement.

Section 1: Create a Retirement Budget

As you embark on your retirement planning journey, estimating your retirement expenses is a pivotal step towards securing a financially comfortable future.

Creating a detailed retirement budget empowers you to gain a comprehensive understanding of the funds needed to maintain your desired lifestyle during your golden years.

In this section, we will see the process of creating a retirement budget, identifying key expense categories tailored to you , and considering the impact of inflation on your future expenses.

Identifying Key Expense Categories

To construct a robust retirement budget, it is essential to identify the key expense categories that will encompass various aspects of your life during retirement.

Here are the primary expense categories

Daily Living Costs:

Groceries: Estimate your monthly grocery expenses based on your current spending patterns and consider any potential changes in dietary needs as you age.

Utilities: Account for ongoing utility bills, such as electricity, water, and gas, taking into consideration potential energy-efficient upgrades in your home.

Transportation: Factor in costs related to maintaining your vehicle, fuel, public transportation, or ride-sharing services.

Healthcare:

Health Insurance Premiums: Estimate your health insurance premiums, including Medicare premiums, and be aware of potential changes in coverage or deductibles.

Medical Expenses: Consider potential out-of-pocket medical expenses, such as copays, prescriptions, and medical treatments.

Housing:

Mortgage or Rent: Include your housing costs, whether it's a mortgage payment or rent, and be mindful of potential changes in housing arrangements as you age.

Property Taxes: Account for property taxes that may fluctuate over time based on local regulations and property values.

Home Maintenance: Budget for routine home maintenance and possible renovations or modifications for aging in place.

Leisure Activities:

Hobbies and Interests: Allocate funds for activities and hobbies you wish to pursue during retirement, such as golf, gardening, or joining clubs.

Entertainment: Consider expenses related to cultural events, movies, dining out, or other leisure activities you enjoy.

Travel:

Vacation and Travel: Plan for your travel aspirations, whether it's exploring new destinations, visiting family, or taking dream vacations.

Charitable Contributions:

Philanthropy: If charitable giving is important to you, allocate a portion of your budget for donations to causes you support.

Miscellaneous Expenses:

Unforeseen Costs: Set aside a buffer for unexpected expenses or emergencies, as life can be full of surprises.

Consider Inflation

Inflation is a vital factor to consider when estimating your retirement expenses. Over time, the cost of goods and services typically increases, which can erode the purchasing power of your retirement income.

To ensure your retirement budget remains accurate and effective, it's crucial to account for inflation in your calculations.

For instance, let's say your current monthly expenses are $5,000. Assuming an average inflation rate of 2.5% annually, in ten years, the same expenses would cost approximately $6,382.

Over twenty years, it would amount to about $8,135. By factoring in inflation, you can better plan for the rising costs of living and ensure your budget is resilient to economic changes.

Practical Exercise: Creating a Retirement Budget

In this section, we will take a step by step to the process of creating a retirement budget, identifying key expense categories, and considering the impact of inflation on your future expenses.

To get started, Identifying Key Expense Categories

Daily Living Costs:

Groceries: Estimate your monthly grocery expenses based on your current spending patterns and consider any potential changes in dietary needs as you age. For example, assume you currently spend an average of $600 per month on groceries.

Utilities: Account for ongoing utility bills, such as electricity, water, and gas, taking into consideration potential energy-efficient upgrades in your home. Assume your monthly utility expenses are approximately $250.

Transportation: Factor in costs related to maintaining your vehicle, fuel, public transportation, or ride-sharing services. If you spend around $200 per month on transportation currently, include this amount in your budget.

Healthcare:

Health Insurance Premiums: Estimate your health insurance premiums, including Medicare premiums, and be aware of potential changes in coverage or deductibles. Assume your monthly health insurance premium is $350.

Medical Expenses: Consider potential out-of-pocket medical expenses, such as copays, prescriptions, and medical treatments. Add an estimated $200 per month to account for medical expenses.

Housing:

Mortgage or Rent: Include your housing costs, whether it's a mortgage payment or rent, and be mindful of potential changes in housing arrangements as you age. If your monthly housing costs are $1,500, include this amount in your budget.

Property Taxes: Account for property taxes that may fluctuate over time based on local regulations and property values. Assuming your property taxes amount to $200 per month, include this expense in your budget.

Home Maintenance: Budget for routine home maintenance and possible renovations or modifications for aging in place. Assume an estimated $150 per month for home maintenance costs.

Leisure Activities:

Hobbies and Interests: Allocate funds for activities and hobbies you wish to pursue during retirement, such as golf, gardening, or joining clubs. If your hobbies and leisure activities cost approximately $300 per month, include this amount in your budget.

Entertainment: Consider expenses related to cultural events, movies, dining out, or other leisure activities you enjoy. Assuming you spend around $150 per month on entertainment, add this expense to your budget.

Travel:

Vacation and Travel: Plan for your travel aspirations, whether it's exploring new destinations, visiting family, or taking dream vacations. If you budget around $300 per month for travel, include this amount in your retirement budget.

Charitable Contributions:

Philanthropy: If charitable giving is important to you, allocate a portion of your budget for donations to causes you support. For example, if you donate $100 per month to charities, include this expense in your budget.

Miscellaneous Expenses:

Unforeseen Costs: Set aside a buffer for unexpected expenses or emergencies, as life can be full of surprises. Including an estimated $100 per month for miscellaneous expenses will provide you with a safety net in your budget.

Consider Inflation

Inflation is a vital factor to consider when estimating your retirement expenses. Over time, the cost of goods and services typically increases, which can erode the purchasing power of your retirement income. To plan effectively, assume a reasonable inflation rate, typically around 2% to 3%, and apply it to each expense category in your budget.

For example, let's assume you plan for retirement in 20 years, and the current inflation rate is 2.5% annually. If your total current monthly expenses (excluding inflation) amount to $3,500, you can estimate your future monthly expenses using the following formula:

Future Monthly Expenses = Current Monthly Expenses * (1 + Inflation Rate) ^ Number of Years

Future Monthly Expenses = $3,500 * (1 + 0.025) ^ 20

Future Monthly Expenses = $3,500 * 1.648

Future Monthly Expenses ≈ $5,772

By factoring in inflation, you can better plan for the rising costs of living and ensure your budget remains resilient to economic changes over time.

Sample: Retirement Budget Worksheet

To guide you through the process of estimating your retirement expenses, we have prepared a comprehensive retirement budget worksheet to help you.

This worksheet will help you itemize and categorize your expected expenses during retirement, providing you with a clear and detailed overview of your financial needs.

[Retirement Budget Worksheet Example]

Let's take an example from the retirement budget worksheet: Susan, aged 55, is planning for her retirement. After assessing her current living costs, she anticipates needing $6,000 per month to maintain her desired lifestyle during retirement.

Considering a 2.5% inflation rate, Susan projects that she will require approximately $8,168 per month in twenty years.

Summary of Monthly Expenses Before and After Inflation:

Let's calculate Susan's estimated monthly expenses during retirement, factoring in inflation to see how her expenses might change in the future.

1. Monthly Expenses Before Inflation:

Susan's estimated monthly expenses before factoring in inflation are $6,000.

2. Monthly Expenses After Inflation (Estimated for Retirement):

Considering a 2.5% inflation rate, we can calculate Susan's projected monthly expenses during retirement as follows:

Future Monthly Expenses = Current Monthly Expenses * (1 + Inflation Rate)^Number of Years

Assuming Susan plans for retirement in 20 years:

Future Monthly Expenses = $6,000 * (1 + 0.025)^20

Future Monthly Expenses = $6,000 * 1.648

Future Monthly Expenses ≈ $9,888

Therefore, based on a 2.5% inflation rate over 20 years, Susan's estimated monthly expenses during retirement would be approximately $9,888.

Conclusion:

After factoring in a 2.5% inflation rate, Susan's projected monthly expenses during retirement would be around $9,888.

It's essential for Susan and anyone planning for retirement to account for inflation in their budgeting to ensure they have sufficient funds to maintain their desired lifestyle throughout their golden years.

By planning ahead and being mindful of inflation's impact, you can make informed financial decisions and create a solid retirement plan that aligns with your goals and aspirations.

CHAPTER 5

Determining Your Annual Retirement Income Goal

I n this chapter, we will delve into the process of determining your retirement income goal.

It is a crucial step in retirement planning as it empowers you to calculate the total amount of money needed annually to maintain your desired lifestyle during retirement.

We will guide you through the steps of setting achievable and specific retirement income goals, ensuring that you can enjoy your golden years with financial security and peace of mind.

Section 1: Assess Existing Retirement Income Sources

It is essential to assess your existing sources of retirement income. Understanding where your income will come from during your golden years will provide you with a clear picture of your current financial situation and help you make informed decisions to ensure a secure and comfortable retirement.

1. Government Benefits:

The first step in assessing your retirement income sources is to look into government benefits that you may be eligible for. In many countries, there are social security programs and other government-sponsored benefits designed to support retirees.

These benefits can include a pension or retirement income that you are entitled to receive based on your years of employment and contributions to the social security system.

Action Steps:

- Contact your local government agency responsible for retirement benefits to inquire about the specific benefits available to you.
- Determine the eligibility criteria and the estimated amount you can expect to receive based on your work history.

2. Employer-Provided Pension Plans:

If you have been part of an employer-sponsored pension plan during your working years, now is the time to examine the details of the plan.

Employer pensions can provide a significant portion of your retirement income, depending on the terms of the plan and the length of your employment.

Action Steps:

- Obtain the pension plan documents from your former or current employer.
- Review the plan details, including the pension benefit formula, vesting requirements, and the age at which you can start receiving benefits.

3. Personal Investments:

Assessing your personal investments is another crucial aspect of determining your retirement income sources.

Personal investments can include savings accounts, individual retirement accounts (IRAs), 401(k)s, stocks, bonds, and real estate properties. These investments can supplement your retirement income and contribute to your financial security during your retirement years.

Action Steps:

- Gather all relevant documents related to your personal investments, such as account statements and investment portfolios.
- Evaluate the current value of each investment and estimate the income they are likely to generate during retirement.

4. Other Income Sources:

Aside from government benefits, employer pensions, and personal investments, there may be other sources of income that you can tap into during retirement.

For example, you might have rental properties, annuities, or part-time employment that can contribute to your retirement income.

Action Steps:

- Make a list of any additional income sources you anticipate during retirement.
- Estimate the income each source is expected to generate and consider how it fits into your overall retirement income plan.

By assessing your existing retirement income sources, you will gain valuable insights into your current financial standing.

This understanding will serve as a foundation for the next steps in your retirement planning journey.

Armed with this knowledge, you will be better prepared to optimize your retirement income and bridge any income gaps, ensuring a fulfilling and financially stable retirement.

Section 2: Explore Additional Income Sources

It's essential to explore additional income sources that can supplement your existing retirement funds.

Diversifying your income streams can provide greater financial security and help bridge any income gaps identified during the Income Gap Analysis exercise.

1, Personal Pension Plans:

Personal pension plans, also known as private pensions or annuities, are financial products offered by financial institutions or insurance companies.

These plans provide regular income payments during retirement, either for a fixed period or for the rest of your life. By purchasing a personal pension plan, you can create a reliable source of income that complements your other retirement funds.

Action Steps:

- Research different personal pension plans available in the market.
- Consider consulting a financial advisor to determine the most suitable plan for your needs and financial goals.

2. Rental Properties:

If you own rental properties, they can serve as a valuable source of retirement income. Rental income can provide a steady stream of cash flow to support your lifestyle during retirement.

Additionally, real estate properties may appreciate in value over time, offering potential long-term benefits.

Action Steps:

- Evaluate the rental income potential of your properties and ensure they are well-maintained to attract tenants.
- Consider the tax implications and expenses associated with managing rental properties.

3. Dividend-Paying Stocks:

Investing in dividend-paying stocks can be an effective way to generate passive income during retirement.

Dividends are periodic payments made by companies to their shareholders, providing you with a share of the company's profits. Reinvesting dividends can further enhance your investment growth.

Action Steps:

- Research and identify dividend-paying companies with a history of consistent dividends.
- Diversify your stock portfolio to minimize risk.

4. Part-Time Employment:

Retirement doesn't necessarily mean you have to stop working altogether. Many retirees choose to work part-time to stay active, engaged, and supplement their retirement income.

Part-time employment can be in your current field or something completely new that aligns with your interests.

Action Steps:

- Explore part-time job opportunities in your local community or online platforms.
- Assess the impact of part-time income on your retirement lifestyle and financial goals.

5. Other Investments:

Aside from traditional retirement accounts and stocks, there are various investment opportunities to explore.

These can include bonds, mutual funds, real estate investment trusts (REITs), or peer-to-peer lending platforms.

Each investment option comes with its own risk and return profile, so it's essential to research and understand them thoroughly.

Action Steps:

- Consult with a financial advisor to assess the suitability of different investment options for your retirement portfolio.
- Consider your risk tolerance and investment objectives before making investment decisions.

By exploring additional income sources, you can strengthen your retirement income strategy and create a well-rounded financial plan.

Diversifying your income streams not only provides stability but also increases the likelihood of achieving your retirement goals.

With careful consideration and prudent decision-making, you can optimize your retirement income and enjoy a fulfilling and worry-free retirement.

Section 3: Determining Your Annual Retirement Income Goal

In this crucial section, we will explore the process of determining your annual retirement income goal—the amount you need to maintain your desired lifestyle during your golden years.

Calculating this goal is a pivotal step in your retirement planning journey, as it lays the foundation for creating a secure and fulfilling retirement tailored to your unique aspirations and needs.

Step 1: Estimate Your Retirement Expenses

To determine your annual retirement income goal, the first step is to estimate your expected retirement expenses.

Your retirement expenses will encompass various categories, including daily living costs, healthcare, housing, leisure activities, travel, and other potential expenditures.

It is essential to be thorough and realistic in your estimates, as this will form the basis for your retirement income calculations.

Example:

Let's say you estimate your total retirement expenses to be $70,000 per year. This includes all your anticipated costs, such as housing ($20,000), healthcare ($10,000), leisure activities ($15,000), daily living expenses ($20,000), and travel ($5,000).

Step 2: Consider Your Retirement Lifestyle

Let's reflect on the discussions in Chapter 2, where you created your retirement vision board.

Take a moment to revisit the dreams, goals, and aspirations you carefully curated for your golden years. Whether it involves traveling the world, pursuing beloved hobbies, cherishing quality time with loved ones, or indulging in new experiences, these elements form the essence of your retirement dreams.

Step 3: Factor in Inflation

Inflation is an essential factor to consider when determining your annual retirement income goal.

Over time, the cost of living typically increases, and your purchasing power may decrease. Factoring in inflation will ensure that your retirement income remains sufficient to cover your expenses throughout your retirement years.

Example:

Assuming an average inflation rate of 2.5%, you would need to adjust your annual retirement expenses accordingly. If your current expenses are $70,000 per year, in 20 years, you would need approximately $117,252 to maintain the same lifestyle due to inflation.

Step 4: Account for Social Security and Other Income Sources

Next, take into account any guaranteed sources of retirement income, such as Social Security benefits and employer pensions. Just As discussed in Section 1 and 2 of this chapter.

These income sources will contribute to your total retirement income and can help reduce the amount you need to generate from your personal savings and investments.

Example:

Suppose you expect to receive $20,000 per year from Social Security and an additional $15,000 from an employer pension. Subtracting these amounts from your annual retirement expenses, your remaining income goal is $82,252 ($117,252 - $20,000 - $15,000).

Step 5: Calculate Your Annual Retirement Income Goal

Now that you have estimated your retirement expenses, factored in inflation, and accounted for other income sources, it's time to calculate your annual retirement income goal—the amount you need to generate from your personal savings and investments.

Example:

Using the previous example, your annual retirement income goal would be $82,252. This is the total amount you need to cover your retirement expenses and maintain your desired lifestyle throughout your golden years.

By going through this process, you gain a comprehensive understanding of the annual income required to support your retirement lifestyle. detailed in your calculations.

With a clear and well-calculated annual retirement income goal, you are well on your way to achieving your retirement dreams with confidence and peace of mind.

Practical Exercise: Determining Your Annual Retirement Income Goal and Gap Analysis.

In this crucial section, we will guide you step-by-step through the process of determining your annual retirement income goal—the amount you need to maintain your desired lifestyle during retirement.

By calculating the total amount of money needed annually to cover your expenses, you will ensure a secure and fulfilling retirement.

Additionally, we will perform a Gap Analysis to assess the difference between your retirement income goal and your existing sources of retirement income. Let's take a detailed journey to a financially sound retirement plan tailored just for you.

Step 1: Assess Your Retirement Expenses

1. Create a Detailed Retirement Budget: Begin by crafting a comprehensive retirement budget that outlines all your expected expenses during retirement. Consider various categories, such as housing costs, healthcare expenses, daily living costs, leisure activities, travel, and any other potential expenditures you foresee.

This budget will be the foundation of your retirement planning and will help you gain clarity on your financial needs during retirement.

For example, you may estimate your annual housing expenses to be $18,000, healthcare costs to be $6,000, daily living expenses to be $12,000, and allocate $10,000 for travel and leisure activities.

2. Consider Your Retirement Lifestyle: Reflect on your retirement goals and the lifestyle you envision for your golden years. Think about the activities, hobbies, and experiences you want to pursue during retirement. Consider how these aspirations may impact your expenses and make adjustments accordingly.

For example, you may decide to allocate an additional $8,000 annually for your retirement lifestyle choices, such as taking up a new hobby and traveling.

3. Factor in Inflation: Account for the impact of inflation on your future expenses. Over time, the cost of living tends to increase, affecting the purchasing power of your money. For conservative planning, let's assume an inflation rate of 2.5% per year.

Example: If you're planning for retirement 20 years from now, your expenses may increase significantly due to inflation. In the first five years, your estimated expenses would grow as follows:

- Year 1: $54,000
- Year 2: $54,000 + ($54,000 * 0.025) = $55,350
- Year 3: $55,350 + ($55,350 * 0.025) = $56,722.88
- Year 4: $56,722.88 + ($56,722.88 * 0.025) = $58,117.39
- Year 5: $58,117.39 + ($58,117.39 * 0.025) = $59,533.91

Step 2: Calculate Your Retirement Income Goal

Total Your Retirement Expenses: Add up all the estimated expenses from Step 1. In this case, your total estimated expenses would be $18,000 + $6,000 + $12,000 + $10,000 + $8,000 = $54,000 per year.

Factor in Inflation: To account for inflation over the next 20 years, apply the inflation rate to your total estimated expenses.

Example: In the fifth year of retirement, your estimated expenses would be $59,533.91.

Step 3: Assess Existing Retirement Income Sources

Determine Guaranteed Sources of Income: Evaluate any guaranteed sources of retirement income you expect to receive, such as Social Security benefits, pensions, or rental income. Estimate the annual amount you will receive from each of these sources.

Example: You anticipate receiving $20,000 annually from Social Security benefits and $10,000 from a pension plan.

Calculate the Income Gap: Subtract the annual amounts you expect to receive from guaranteed sources from your total estimated expenses. The result will be the income you need to generate from your personal savings and investments.

Example: Total income from Social Security benefits and a pension plan is $20,000 + $10,000 = $30,000. Therefore, you would need to generate an additional $29,533.91 annually from your savings and investments.

Step 4: Perform Gap Analysis

Compare Income Goal with Current Savings: Now that you have calculated your retirement income goal, assess your existing retirement savings. Determine if your current savings are sufficient to meet your income goal during retirement.

Example: If your retirement income goal in the fifth year of retirement is $59,533.91, and your expected income from Social Security and pensions is $30,000, you would need to generate an additional $29,533.91 annually from your savings and investments.

Identify Any Shortfalls: If there is a gap between your retirement income goal and your current savings, you have an income shortfall. This means you need to take additional steps to bridge the gap and ensure a secure retirement.

Step 5: Adjust Your Retirement Plan

Explore Savings and Investment Strategies: To bridge the income gap and achieve your retirement income goal, consider different savings and investment strategies.

For example, you may decide to increase your contributions to retirement accounts, such as an Individual Retirement Account (IRA) or 401(k), to accelerate your savings growth.

Revisit Your Retirement Lifestyle: If your income goal seems challenging to achieve, review your retirement lifestyle choices and consider adjustments to align your expenses with your financial capacity.

Finding a balance between your dreams and financial reality is crucial for long-term financial security.

By completing this practical exercise and performing the Gap Analysis, you will have a comprehensive understanding of your retirement income needs.

Armed with this knowledge, you can make informed decisions and take appropriate actions to achieve your retirement goals.

Remember that personalized advice from financial professionals can provide tailored insights to optimize your retirement plan. Planning for retirement may seem daunting, but with the right guidance and careful analysis, you can confidently build a financial strategy that ensures a fulfilling and worry-free retirement journey.

Calculating Monthly Retirement Contributions

In this section, we will see the process of determining the specific amount of money you need to contribute on a monthly basis to bridge the retirement income gap.

By following this step-by-step guide and using real-life examples and scenarios, you will gain a comprehensive understanding of how to calculate your monthly retirement contributions with confidence.

Step 1: Review Your Retirement Income Goal and Expenses

First, let's revisit your annual retirement income goal from Section 1. For example, if your retirement income goal in the fifth year of retirement is $59,533.91, and you expect to receive $30,000 from Social Security and pensions, you would need to generate an additional $29,533.91 annually from your savings and investments to meet your goal.

Step 2: Assess Your Retirement Investment Options

Before calculating your monthly retirement contributions, let's explore the different investment options available to you. Retirement accounts, such as Individual Retirement Accounts (IRAs) and 401(k)s, offer tax advantages and long-term growth potential. Stocks, bonds, and mutual funds are also common investment choices with varying levels of risk and return.

Example: Let's say you decide to invest in a retirement account with an expected annual return of 6%. Now, it's time to calculate your monthly contributions to meet the income shortfall.

Step 3: Determine Your Monthly Contribution

To calculate your monthly retirement contribution, you need to divide the annual income shortfall by the number of months in a year.

Example: Using the previous example, your annual income shortfall is $29,533.91. So, to find the monthly contribution needed, you perform the following calculation:

Monthly Contribution = Annual Income Shortfall / 12

Monthly Contribution = $29,533.91 / 12

Monthly Contribution = $2,461.16

This means you would need to contribute approximately $2,461.16 each month to bridge the income gap and reach your retirement income goal.

Step 4: Optimize Your Retirement Savings

Once you've determined your monthly contribution, consider strategies to optimize your retirement savings. If your current budget allows, you may consider increasing your monthly contributions to accelerate your savings growth.

Additionally, take advantage of employer-sponsored retirement plans, such as a 401(k), especially if your employer offers matching contributions. This can provide a significant boost to your retirement savings.

Step 5: Monitor and Adjust Your Plan

As you start making monthly contributions, regularly monitor your retirement plan's progress. Review your investment performance, and make adjustments as needed to stay on track with your retirement income goal.

Life circumstances may change, so it's essential to reassess your retirement plan periodically.

If your financial situation improves, you may choose to increase your contributions further or explore additional investment opportunities.

Conclusion:

By completing this chapter and understanding how to calculate your monthly retirement contributions, you are now equipped with a solid plan to achieve your retirement goals.

Remember that personalized advice from financial professionals can provide tailored insights to optimize your retirement plan and lead you toward a brighter financial future.

CHAPTER 6

Supplement Retirement Savings with Other Investments

Welcome to Chapter 6, where we take a crucial step in your retirement planning journey: exploring the world of additional investments to supplement your retirement savings.

We have already laid the groundwork by assessing your existing sources of income and identifying any gaps. Now, it's time to expand your financial horizons and make informed decisions that will fortify your retirement nest egg.

In the previous chapters, we discussed the significance of personal pension plans and evaluated your current financial standing.

Armed with this knowledge, you are now ready to explore a diverse range of investment opportunities that can enhance your retirement prospects.

This chapter will be your guide to understanding various investment options, assessing their risks and rewards, and aligning them with your retirement goals.

Remember, the journey to a secure retirement is not just about saving; it's about making wise choices that will maximize your financial potential.

Diversify your investments.

Now, you might wonder, why is diversification so crucial?" Well, my dear readers, let me tell you that diversification is like the key that unlocks the door to financial stability and growth.

It's the secret sauce that ensures your retirement plan remains strong even in the face of unpredictable market twists and turns.

So, let's get right into it, shall we? Investment diversification is the art of spreading your hard-earned money across a variety of financial vehicles, each with its own unique features and potential.

Just like planting a diversified garden, you want a mix of assets that can weather different climates and seasons.

By doing so, you're building a robust portfolio that mitigates risk and maximizes the potential for returns.

Diversification is like a shield protecting you from the unpredictability of financial markets.

Picture this: if one investment takes a tumble, there's another standing tall to catch you and soften the blow. It's all about creating a well-rounded financial foundation that stands strong, no matter what.

Benefits of investment diversification

Now, let's explore the wonderful benefits of investment diversification:

Risk Mitigation: We can't predict the future, but we can certainly prepare for it. Diversification spreads your investments across various asset classes, so you're not putting all your eggs in one basket.

Some days, the market might frown upon your stocks, but fear not, for your bonds and real estate investments will lend a hand in balancing the scales.

Improved Tax Efficiency: Smart diversification can help you keep more of your hard-earned money in your pocket.

By carefully selecting tax-efficient accounts like Roth IRAs and 401(k)s, you can optimize your savings and enjoy tax-free income during your golden years.

Enhanced Income Streams: Ah, the sweet sound of cash flowing in! With diversification, you're not just relying on one income stream; you've got a symphony of cash coming in from different sources.

From dividend-paying stocks to rental income, each note contributes to your financial harmony.

Steps to Diversifying Investment

Now, let's get down to business and walk you through the steps of diversifying your investment portfolio:

Step 1: Assess Your Risk Tolerance: Take a deep breath and understand your risk tolerance.

How much risk can you handle? Be honest with yourself, for this step is the foundation of your diversified portfolio.

Are you ready to embrace a bit of excitement, or do you prefer a more conservative approach? Once you know your comfort level, you can proceed with confidence.

Step 2: Allocate Across Asset Classes: Now that you know your risk tolerance, it's time to spread the love.

Allocate your investments across various asset classes, like stocks, bonds, real estate, and alternative investments. Each asset class dances to a different beat, adding its own flair to your portfolio.

Step 3: Select Individual Investments Wisely: Like picking ripe fruit, choose your individual investments wisely. Look for companies with solid fundamentals and growth potential. Research, and research.

Step 4: Rebalance Regularly: Life is ever-changing, and so is your portfolio. Regularly check in and rebalance your investments to ensure they stay true to your intended diversification strategy.

Step 5: Embrace Tax-Efficient Accounts Optimize your savings by embracing tax-efficient accounts like Roth IRAs and 401(k)s. Remember, you deserve to reap the rewards of your hard work without unnecessary tax burdens.

Embrace the Power of Real Estate and Income-Generating Assets

This is a realm of financial wisdom that can add strength and resilience to your retirement nest egg.

Why venture into the world of real estate, you might wonder?

Benefits

Steady Income Stream: Imagine having a gentle river of income flowing into your life, soothing any financial worries that may linger.

Real estate investments, particularly rental properties, offer just that! By leasing out properties, you can generate a steady and reliable stream of rental income to support your retirement lifestyle.

Hedge Against Inflation: As we journey through the years, inflation may raise its head, chipping away at the purchasing power of your money.

But fear not, for real estate can be a shield against this monetary dance. Rental income has the potential to rise with inflation, ensuring that your income keeps pace with the ever-changing cost of living.

Tangible Asset: There's an undeniable satisfaction in owning a tangible piece of land or property, a canvas that you can see, touch, and cherish.

Unlike intangible investments, such as stocks or bonds, real estate allows you to feel the presence of your asset. Moreover, it offers the added benefit of potential capital appreciation over time, building wealth for your golden years.

Action Steps

Step 1: Define Your Investment Strategy Just as an artist envisions their masterpiece, you too must envision your investment strategy.

Consider your risk tolerance, desired income level, and time horizon. Are you inclined towards a hands-on approach, or would you prefer a more passive investment style? This clarity will guide you down the right path.

Step 2: Research, Research, Research! As you tread upon this path, arm yourself with knowledge!

Delve into extensive research to understand the local real estate market, property types, rental demand, and potential growth prospects. Knowledge is your greatest asset in making informed investment decisions.

Step 3: Build a Diverse Real Estate Portfolio: Much like a gardener sows a variety of seeds, you too must sow diversity in your real estate portfolio.

Consider investing in different types of properties, such as residential, commercial, or vacation rentals.

Each property type offers unique benefits and risks, so embrace the balance that suits your aspirations and risk tolerance.

Step 4: Finance Wisely Just as a prudent chef balances flavors, you too must find the right financial mix.

Evaluate your options for financing real estate investments, such as mortgages, and choose the ones that align with your long-term goals.

Remember to consider interest rates, terms, and repayment plans to ensure you are making sound financial choices.

Step 5: Property Management: As you embark on this real estate journey, consider your role as a landlord.

Are you prepared to manage properties yourself, or would you prefer to enlist the help of a property management company?

Efficient management is the key to a successful and stress-free investment experience.

They diligently researched the best locations and managed the properties with care.

Over time, they enjoyed a steady stream of rental income, which provided them with financial comfort and allowed them to pursue their passion for travel during retirement.

Avoid Using Pension Funds as Collateral for Loans

While it may seem like a convenient option, leveraging your pension for short-term gains can have severe long-term consequences.

In this section, we will explore the risks associated with using pension funds as collateral and why it is best to avoid this practice.

1. Jeopardizing Retirement Security

Your pension is an essential pillar of your retirement security, providing a steady stream of income during your golden years.

By using it as collateral for loans, you put your future financial stability at risk. Any default on the loan could lead to the loss of a significant portion of your pension, leaving you with diminished retirement income.

Protecting your pension is crucial for maintaining a comfortable lifestyle and meeting your financial needs during retirement.

2. Penalties and Taxes

Using pension funds as collateral can expose you to unnecessary tax liabilities and early withdrawal penalties. Retirement accounts, such as 401(k)s or IRAs, offer tax advantages and are designed to encourage long-term savings.

Prematurely tapping into these funds can trigger additional taxes and penalties, eroding the value of your retirement savings and reducing their potential for growth.

3. Potential Debt Spiral

Taking on additional debt by using pension funds as collateral may lead to a dangerous cycle of borrowing.

If you are unable to repay the loan, you might resort to taking out more loans, exacerbating your financial strain.

This debt spiral can quickly spiral out of control, making it challenging to recover financially and jeopardizing your overall financial health.

4. Lack of Diversification

Diversification is a fundamental principle of sound financial planning. By using your pension funds as collateral, you may be concentrating too much risk in a single investment, potentially leading to significant losses if the investment does not perform as expected.

Diversifying your investment portfolio allows you to spread risk across different assets and increase the likelihood of achieving long-term financial goals.

5. Limited Access to Retirement Funds

Using your pension funds as collateral can limit your access to emergency funds during times of financial hardship.

These funds are meant to be a safety net for unexpected expenses or medical emergencies. By tying up your pension in a loan, you may find yourself ill-prepared to handle financial emergencies, leading to further stress and financial strain.

Practical Exercise: Crafting Your Investment Strategy for a Rewarding Retirement

In this section, we're going to learn how to create a plan for your money that fits how comfortable you are with taking risks.

Step 1: Assess Your Risk Tolerance and Embrace Your Unique Financial Comfort Zone

To begin, we must first understand your risk tolerance—the very essence of how you feel about the ups and downs of the financial markets.

Close your eyes and imagine the emotional response you have when your investments face market fluctuations. Are you at ease with the idea of short-term losses in pursuit of long-term gains, or do you prefer a more conservative approach that prioritizes the preservation of your hard-earned capital?

Step 2: Set Clear Financial Goals—Your Roadmap to Financial Freedom

Next, let us revisit the financial goals you have diligently crafted in Chapter 3. These goals serve as your guiding beacons, illuminating the path to your ideal retirement. Ensure your goals remain specific, measurable, achievable, relevant, and time-bound (SMART) to keep you focused on the destination.

Step 3: Diversify Your Portfolio: The Pillar of Financial Resilience

Diversification is the key to building a robust investment strategy. By spreading your investments across various asset classes, you safeguard your portfolio from the undue impact of any single investment. Consider a thoughtful mix of stocks, bonds, real estate, and other investment vehicles tailored to your risk tolerance and financial goals.

Step 4: Research and Select Investments: Empowering Informed Decisions

With your risk tolerance, financial goals, and diversification strategy in mind, it is time to embark on thorough research and select specific investments. Delve deep into the performance history, expense ratios, and management team of potential investment options. Seek investments with a proven track record of delivering consistent returns and aligning with your investment philosophy.

As you conduct your research, you discover a mutual fund that aligns perfectly with your risk tolerance, boasts low expense ratios, and is managed by a seasoned team with a history of delivering solid returns. You confidently add this fund to your portfolio, knowing it aligns with your long-term objectives.

Step 5: Monitor and Rebalance: The Journey of Continuous Optimization

Remember, that an investment strategy is not a static blueprint but a dynamic journey. Regularly monitor your portfolio's performance and rebalance as needed to maintain your desired asset allocation. Market fluctuations and changes in your financial situation may shift your portfolio's composition, necessitating adjustments to stay on course.

As you approach retirement, revisit your portfolio annually to ensure it remains aligned with your goals. Adjust the allocation slightly, increasing your bond holdings for added stability in preparation for your transition to retirement.

Step 6: Seek Professional Advice: The Guiding Hand of Expertise

While you have taken significant strides in crafting your investment strategy, seeking advice from a financial advisor can provide invaluable insights and an unbiased perspective. An experienced advisor can ensure your investment choices align with your long-term objectives and provide guidance as you traverse your financial landscape.

When you consult a financial advisor, you find their applause for your investment strategy reassuring. They suggest a few minor tweaks to optimize your portfolio further. Their expert guidance instills confidence as you embark on your retirement journey.

In conclusion, dear readers, developing a prudent investment strategy is the hallmark of a well-prepared retirement.

By assessing your risk tolerance, setting clear financial goals, diversifying your portfolio, researching investments, and seeking professional advice, you take charge of your financial destiny.

Connect the knowledge from previous chapters to this transformative exercise, and let wisdom be your guide as you forge ahead.

Remember that each investment decision brings you closer to the enchanting retirement you've envisioned.

Embrace the power of compounding growth and the resilience of diversification to safeguard your financial future.

Onward we go, my dear readers, to embrace the captivating possibilities of a fulfilling retirement journey!

CHAPTER 7

Continuously Monitor and Adjust

The power of adaptability, and the rewards of staying proactive on your financial journey.

Together, we will explore why continuous monitoring is the linchpin to your retirement success and how making timely adjustments can bring you closer to the fulfilling retirement you've envisioned.

Life is a beautiful journey filled with unexpected twists and turns, and your financial strategy must remain agile to navigate through any surprises that come your way.

By actively monitoring your progress, staying informed about investment opportunities, and seeking professional advice, you will fortify your retirement dreams and ensure a prosperous and fulfilling future.

The Dynamic Nature of Life and Finance

Life is ever-changing, and retirement planning is no exception.

Just as the seasons shift and the tides rise and fall, your financial goals and priorities may evolve as you journey through different life stages.

That's why it is crucial to embrace the dynamic nature of life and recognize that your retirement plan is not a static document but a living, breathing roadmap.

Regular reviews empower you to ensure your financial strategy grows and adapts alongside you, reflecting your current aspirations and circumstances.

Regularly reviewing your plan allows you to seize opportunities and align your strategy with your evolving goals.

The Benefits of Regular Reviews

Regular reviews of your retirement plan offer an array of benefits. It's like taking your financial pulse regularly to ensure your money is working as hard as you are.

By conducting these assessments, you can track your progress towards your financial objectives, celebrate milestones achieved, and detect any potential gaps that may require your attention.

Suppose you've been diligently saving for retirement, contributing to your employer's retirement plan, and consistently investing in diverse assets.

Regularly reviewing your progress may reveal that you've reached a significant milestone, like accumulating $500,000 in your retirement accounts. This achievement should be celebrated as a testament to your dedication and discipline.

Keep a Watchful Eye on Investment Opportunities

Diversifying your investment portfolio is a critical element of a robust retirement strategy.

While you've already laid the groundwork in previous chapters, it's essential to continue staying informed about new investment opportunities that align with your risk tolerance and financial goals.

Additionally, staying informed about changes in economic conditions and market trends can empower you to make informed decisions.

Economic fluctuations and geopolitical events can impact your investment portfolio, and understanding these factors helps you navigate through uncertainties with confidence.

The Impact of Changing Economic Conditions

Economic conditions are like the wind beneath your financial sails, influencing the markets and shaping your investment returns.

By keeping an eye on economic trends, interest rates, inflation, and geopolitical events, you gain valuable insights to make proactive decisions.

Imagine this: Economic conditions signal an upcoming period of higher inflation. In response, you may consider adjusting your investment allocation to include assets that historically perform well during inflationary times, such as Treasury Inflation-Protected Securities (TIPS).

By doing so, you protect your portfolio from eroding purchasing power and secure a more stable financial future.

The Wisdom of Seeking Professional Advice

The Role of a Financial Advisor

While you are the captain of your retirement ship, a skilled financial advisor can be your trusted navigator.

A financial advisor brings expertise, objectivity, and a broader perspective to the table. Periodically seeking their guidance can help you optimize your retirement strategy and make well-informed decisions in the ever-changing financial landscape.

Suppose you are unsure about which investment options align best with your risk tolerance and financial goals.

A financial advisor can conduct a detailed risk assessment and design a personalized investment strategy tailored to your needs. This guidance empowers you to make choices that resonate with your unique circumstances and aspirations.

Collaboration for Success

Your relationship with your financial advisor is a powerful partnership.

Collaboratively working together allows you to address concerns, explore new opportunities, and implement strategies to overcome challenges.

By seeking periodic advice, you remain proactive in adapting your plan to reflect life's changes and optimize your financial security.

For instance, as you near retirement, you might have questions about the best time to claim Social Security benefits. Your financial advisor can help you navigate the complexities of Social Security rules and strategize the optimal time to begin claiming benefits, maximizing your income stream during retirement.

In conclusion, regularly reviewing your retirement plan, staying informed about investment opportunities, and seeking professional advice are essential pillars of your financial success.

Just as a gardener tends to their plants with care and attention, you must nurture your financial garden continuously.

Your journey to retirement is dynamic and exciting, and with diligent monitoring and prudent adjustments, you can thrive in the ever-changing financial landscape. Embrace the power of continuous review and remain

Practical Exercise: Retirement Plan Review

Welcome to the final phase of your retirement planning journey! In this section, we will delve into a vital practical exercise that can propel you towards a financially secure and fulfilling retirement.

The key to making your dreams a reality lies in the power of regular reviews and adjustments to your retirement plan.

By creating a well-structured schedule for reviewing and updating your strategy, you'll stay on track, adapt to changing circumstances, and make informed decisions in response to fluctuations in the financial markets.

So, let's embark on this transformative exercise and secure your prosperous future!

Step 1: Establish a Review Schedule

The foundation of successful retirement planning lies in consistency and discipline. Just as you schedule regular health check-ups to maintain your well-being, establishing a review schedule for your retirement plan is equally crucial. Determine how often you'll conduct these reviews, considering both your personal preferences and the complexity of your financial situation.

For most individuals, an annual review proves effective. Mark a specific date on your calendar, such as the start of the new year, as your designated review day.

Treating this appointment with yourself as non-negotiable ensures you maintain a proactive approach to your financial well-being.

Step 2: Gather Your Financial Documents

Before each review session, gather all your financial documents in one place. These documents should include your investment account statements, retirement account balances, Social Security estimates, insurance policies, and any other relevant financial records.

Having a comprehensive snapshot of your financial standing empowers you to make informed decisions during the review process.

This step also allows you to track your progress over time, giving you a clear view of how far you've come towards your retirement goals.

Step 3: Assess Your Progress Toward Goals

As you embark on your review, it's essential to assess your progress toward your retirement goals. Revisit the SMART goals you set in earlier chapters, such as the specific amount you want to save for retirement or the age at which you plan to retire.

For instance, let's say one of your goals was to accumulate $750,000 in your retirement accounts by age 65. During the review, you discover that you've saved $600,000 so far.

Take a moment to reflect on the steps you've taken to reach this milestone and consider how you can further increase your savings rate to stay on track.

Step 4: Analyze Investment Performance

The performance of your investment portfolio plays a crucial role in the success of your retirement plan.

During the review, take the time to analyze how each asset class has performed over the past year.

Consider how market fluctuations have impacted your investments and whether your portfolio remains aligned with your risk tolerance and long-term objectives.

For example, if you notice that a particular stock has significantly underperformed, it may be time to consider diversifying your portfolio or reallocating your investments to mitigate risks and optimize returns.

Step 5: Evaluate Life Changes

Life is filled with surprises, and some events may impact your retirement plan. Take a moment to consider any significant life changes that may have occurred since your last review.

Have you experienced a change in employment, received an inheritance, or had a major life event, such as marriage or the birth of a child?

These changes can affect your financial goals and priorities, warranting adjustments to your retirement plan.

For instance, if you recently received an inheritance, you may consider allocating a portion of these funds towards your retirement savings to accelerate your progress.

Step 6: Stay Informed About Economic Conditions

As you conduct your review, stay informed about changing economic conditions and their potential impact on your retirement strategy.

Keep an eye on interest rates, inflation rates, and market trends to make well-informed decisions.

For example, if economic conditions indicate rising inflation rates, you may consider adjusting your investment allocations to include inflation-protected assets that preserve your purchasing power.

Step 7: Seek Professional guidance.

While the review process empowers you to take control of your financial future, seeking professional guidance from a financial advisor can provide invaluable insights and expertise.

Consider meeting with your financial advisor at least once a year, aligned with your review schedule.

A financial advisor can offer personalized recommendations, conduct detailed risk assessments, and help you optimize your retirement strategy.

Step 8: Make Strategic Adjustments

As you complete each review, take note of any adjustments you need to make to your retirement plan.

Whether it's increasing your savings rate, reallocating your investments, or considering new income streams, strategic adjustments are crucial to staying on track.

For instance, if you find that you've fallen behind in achieving your savings goals, you may decide to increase your contributions to your retirement accounts each month.

In conclusion, the practical exercise of creating a retirement plan review schedule is a powerful tool for achieving your financial dreams.

By regularly assessing your progress, staying informed about economic conditions, and seeking professional guidance, you'll maintain control over your financial destiny.

Just as a skilled captain navigates through changing waters, you have the power to adapt and steer your retirement plan to success.

Embrace the practice of continuous monitoring and adjustments, and you'll build a robust retirement strategy that stands the test of time.

Your financial security and fulfilling retirement await you, and with each review, you move closer to turning your dreams into reality.

Remember, it's never too late to take charge of your financial future. So, start today and pave the way for a prosperous tomorrow!

CHAPTER 8

Obtaining Adequate Insurance Coverage - Safeguarding Your Retirement Dreams

Just like building an emergency fund, insurance plays a vital role in safeguarding your retirement dreams.

It acts as a protective shield, providing you and your loved ones with financial support and peace of mind during life's uncertainties.

Throughout our previous chapters, we've explored the essential elements of retirement planning, from creating a realistic savings plan, managing debts, diversifying investments, to building a robust emergency fund.

Now, it's time to fortify your retirement strategy by understanding the different types of insurance, determining your coverage needs, and making informed decisions to ensure your retirement vision remains intact.

In this chapter, we will explore the importance of various insurance policies, how to evaluate your insurance needs, and practical steps to obtain the right coverage.

From health insurance to life insurance, long-term care to disability insurance, we'll cover it all, arming you with the knowledge and tools to make confident insurance choices.

As we transition into the world of insurance, remember that each piece of the retirement puzzle we've discussed thus far plays a crucial role in creating a comprehensive and robust financial plan.

Insurance serves as a protective layer, preventing unforeseen events from derailing your retirement dreams and helping you maintain your financial security throughout your golden years.

Assessing Your Insurance Needs

To begin, let's assess your unique insurance needs, considering your current situation, future goals, and potential risks.

By evaluating these factors, you can determine the appropriate level of coverage for your retirement years. Let's walk through the steps to assess your insurance needs:

Taking Stock of Your Assets and Liabilities:

Start by getting a clear picture of your financial position. Calculate your total assets, including savings, investments, and retirement accounts.

On the other side, identify any outstanding debts, such as mortgages, loans, or credit card balances. Understanding your net worth will help you gauge the level of insurance protection you require to secure your retirement.

For example, let's say you're a couple in your early 50s with retirement savings of $800,000, investments worth $200,000, and a remaining mortgage balance of $100,000. In this case, your net worth is $900,000, and you would want to ensure your insurance coverage accounts for this figure.

Evaluating Your Health and Family Situation:

Your health and family situation are critical factors in determining the types and amount of insurance coverage you might need.

Consider your current health status, any pre-existing medical conditions, and your family's health history. For instance, if you have a family history of certain medical conditions, it may be wise to invest in comprehensive health insurance that covers potential medical expenses related to those conditions.

Additionally, assess your family situation, including dependents, children, or aging parents who may rely on your financial support.

Life insurance can be an essential tool to protect your family's financial well-being in case of your untimely passing.

Analyzing Potential Risks:

Identifying potential risks that could impact your financial security is essential. These risks may include unexpected medical emergencies, disability, loss of income, or premature death. By recognizing these risks, you can tailor your insurance coverage to protect against them effectively.

For instance, if your career involves physical labor or high-risk activities, disability insurance can provide you with an income replacement safety net in case an injury prevents you from working.

Understanding Health, Life, and Long-Term Care Insurance

Now that we've assessed your insurance needs, let's explore the three primary types of insurance coverage: health insurance, life insurance, and long-term care insurance.

1. Health Insurance:

Health insurance is a fundamental aspect of any retirement plan. It is designed to cover medical expenses, ensuring access to quality healthcare without depleting your savings.
Here are some key points to understand about health insurance:
Types of Health Insurance: Familiarize yourself with the different health insurance plans available,

such as Health Maintenance Organizations (HMOs), Preferred Provider Organizations (PPOs), and High-Deductible Health Plans (HDHPs) with Health Savings Accounts (HSAs).

Coverage and Costs: Take a close look at what medical services and treatments are covered by your plan, as well as copayments, deductibles, and out-of-pocket maximums. Assess the costs of premiums and determine the balance between affordability and coverage.

For example, suppose you're approaching retirement and will no longer have employer-sponsored health coverage. In that case, you might explore options like Medicare, which provides health insurance for those aged 65 and older.

2. Life Insurance:

Life insurance serves as financial protection for your loved ones in the event of your passing. Here's what you need to know about life insurance:

Types of Life Insurance: Learn about the two primary types of life insurance—term life insurance and permanent life insurance (whole life and universal life). Each type has unique features and benefits.

Coverage Amount: Calculate the appropriate coverage amount based on your outstanding debts, income replacement needs, and your family's future financial requirements.

For instance, if you still have a mortgage to pay off and your children are not yet financially independent, you might opt for a term life insurance policy with coverage that matches your remaining mortgage balance and provides sufficient funds to support your children until they are self-sufficient.

3. Long-Term Care Insurance:

Long-term care insurance covers the costs of extended care services, such as assisted living or home care, in case you require long-term assistance with daily activities.

Considering the following aspects will help you navigate long-term care insurance:

Coverage Options: Understand the types of long-term care services covered, benefit periods, and elimination periods before benefits kick in.

Cost and Affordability: Evaluate the premiums and ensure the policy fits within your budget while providing adequate coverage.

For example, if you're concerned about potential long-term care expenses affecting your retirement savings, long-term care insurance could be a prudent choice to alleviate that financial burden.

Finding the Right Insurance Policies

With a clear understanding of your insurance needs and the types of coverage available, let's move on to finding the right insurance policies.

Here's a step-by-step approach to help you in the process:

1. Shop Around and Compare Quotes:
Start by obtaining quotes from multiple insurance providers to compare coverage options and premiums. Keep in mind that different insurers may offer varying levels of coverage, and it's essential to find the one that best aligns with your needs.

2. Review Policy Terms and Conditions:

Once you've narrowed down your choices, thoroughly review the policy terms and conditions. Pay close attention to coverage limits, exclusions, and any optional riders that may enhance your protection.

3. Seek Professional Advice:

Insurance can be a complex subject, and seeking advice from a qualified insurance agent or financial advisor can be invaluable. An expert can guide you through the intricacies of insurance and assist you in making informed decisions about your coverage.

4. Reevaluate and Adjust:

As your life circumstances change—such as major life events or reaching retirement milestones—make it a habit to reevaluate your insurance needs regularly. Adjust your coverage as necessary to ensure your insurance policies continue to meet your evolving needs.

Obtaining adequate insurance coverage is a vital component of your retirement planning efforts. By assessing your insurance needs, understanding health, life, and long-term care insurance, and finding the right policies, you can create a solid safety net for your retirement years.

CHAPTER 9

Managing Debts

Welcome to Chapter 9, where we'll explore the world of managing debts—a crucial aspect of your retirement planning journey.

Throughout our previous chapters, we've laid a solid foundation for your retirement plan. We've explored the importance of setting clear financial goals, creating a realistic savings plan, Obtaining adequate insurance coverage, diversifying your investments, and building a well-balanced investment portfolio.

Now, as we continue let's address the often-overlooked but equally significant part of the equation: debt management.

Imagine your financial life as a sailboat. The wind propelling your vessel forward represents your income and savings, while the anchors holding you back are your debts.

To reach your retirement destination smoothly and with ease, it's essential to strike a balance between the two—maximizing the wind's force while minimizing the drag from the anchors.

It's not uncommon to feel a little apprehensive about managing debts, especially as you approach retirement age.

Section 1: Evaluating Your Debt Situation

To get started,

Step 1: Reviewing Your Debt Portfolio

Take a comprehensive look at your existing debts, including credit card balances, loans, and mortgages. Note the outstanding balances, interest rates, and minimum monthly payments for each debt.

Example: Let's consider John, who is 56 years old and planning for retirement. His debt portfolio includes the following:

Credit Card Debt: John has an outstanding balance of $7,000 on his credit card, with an interest rate of 18% and a minimum monthly payment of $200.

Auto Loan: He also has an auto loan with a remaining balance of $15,000, an interest rate of 6%, and a minimum monthly payment of $400.

Mortgage: John's mortgage has a remaining balance of $250,000, an interest rate of 4.5%, and a minimum monthly payment of $1,500.
Step 2: Calculating Total Debt Load

Sum up the total outstanding balance of all your debts. This figure represents the overall size of your debt burden.

Example: John's total debt load is $272,000, which includes credit card debt, an auto loan, and a mortgage.

Step 3: Assessing Debt-to-Income Ratio

Your debt-to-income ratio is a crucial indicator of your financial health. Calculate it by dividing your total monthly debt payments by your monthly income.

Example: If John's total monthly debt payments amount to $2,100, and his monthly income is $6,500, his debt-to-income ratio is approximately 32% ($2,100 / $6,500).

By evaluating your debt situation, you gain a clear understanding of your financial position and can make informed decisions regarding debt management in the context of your retirement goals.

Section 2: Prioritizing Debt Repayment Strategies

Step 1: The Snowball Method

The Snowball Method involves paying off debts in order of smallest to largest balance, regardless of interest rates. Start by allocating any extra funds beyond minimum payments to the smallest debt.

Example: John decides to use the Snowball Method. He allocates an additional $300 each month to his credit card debt, which has the smallest balance.

Step 2: Celebrating Victories

As you pay off the smallest debt, celebrate the victory! This emotional motivation can provide the wind in your sails to tackle the next debt on your list.

Example: After several months of disciplined payments, John successfully pays off his credit card debt. He feels a sense of accomplishment and is motivated to move on to the auto loan.

Step 3: Snowballing Effect

With each debt paid off, the amount available for repayment snowballs. Apply the total payment amount from the first debt to the next smallest debt on your list.

Example: After clearing his credit card debt, John now adds the $300 he was paying on the credit card to his auto loan payment, making a total of $700 per month towards the auto loan.

Step 4: The Avalanche Method

The Avalanche Method involves paying off debts in order of highest to lowest interest rates. Start by allocating any extra funds beyond minimum payments to the debt with the highest interest rate.

Example: After clearing his credit card debt, John shifts his focus to the Avalanche Method. He allocates the additional $300 each month to his auto loan, which has the highest interest rate.

Step 5: Reducing Interest Costs

The Avalanche Method minimizes the overall interest paid on debts, potentially saving you more money in the long run.

Step 6: Finding the Right Balance

You can also use a hybrid approach, combining elements of both the Snowball and Avalanche Methods to strike a balance that works best for your financial situation.

Example: John decides to use a hybrid approach. While he prioritizes paying off his credit card debt first using the Snowball Method, he also allocates some extra funds towards his auto loan to reduce the interest cost using the Avalanche Method.

By prioritizing your debt repayment strategies, you navigate the waters of debt management with confidence and efficiency. As you celebrate victories along the way, remember to connect these principles to the broader context of retirement planning we've discussed throughout this book.

Your journey towards a debt-free retirement is not just about reaching the destination but embracing the process with confidence and determination.

Section 3: Reducing High-Interest Debts

High-interest debts can create rough seas on your path to financial security. To steer clear of turbulent waters, employ strategies to reduce the burden of high-interest debts.

Step 1: Negotiating Lower Interest Rates

Reach out to your creditors and explore the possibility of negotiating lower interest rates on your outstanding debts.

Example: John contacts his credit card company and successfully negotiates a reduced interest rate of 12% on his outstanding balance.

Step 2: Exploring Debt Consolidation

Debt consolidation involves combining multiple debts into a single loan with a lower interest rate. This can simplify your payments and potentially save you money on interest.

Example: John decides to consolidate his credit card debt and auto loan into a single loan with a lower interest rate. This streamlines his debt repayment efforts.

Step 3: Focusing on High-Interest Debts

Allocate any extra funds beyond minimum payments towards high-interest debts. By reducing these debts first, you save money on interest payments.

Example: John makes sure to prioritize his credit card debt, which has the highest interest rate of 12%.

Step 4: Building Emergency Savings

Creating an emergency savings fund can act as a safety net during times of financial uncertainty, reducing the need to rely on high-interest credit cards.

Example: John sets up an emergency savings fund with three to six months' worth of living expenses. This provides him with a financial cushion to avoid high-interest debt during unexpected events.

By reducing high-interest debts, you navigate towards smoother financial waters and position yourself for a secure retirement.

By evaluating your debt situation, prioritizing repayment strategies, and reducing high-interest debts, you take control of your financial destiny.

As you navigate through these debt management waters, remember to connect these principles to the broader context of retirement planning we've discussed throughout this book.

Your journey towards a debt-free retirement is not just about reaching the destination but embracing the process with confidence and determination.

Practical Exercise: Developing Your Debt Payoff Plan

Now, let's dive into the practical side of things and develop a personalized debt payoff plan that will guide you towards a debt-free retirement. Remember, each person's financial situation is unique, so tailor this plan to suit your needs and goals.

Step 1: Gather Your Debt Information

The first step is to gather all the necessary information about your debts. Grab a notepad or open a spreadsheet on your computer to keep track of the details. For each debt, include the following:

Name of the Debt: Identify each debt, such as credit cards, student loans, auto loans, personal loans, or mortgages.

Outstanding Balance: Note down the current outstanding balance for each debt. This is the total amount you still owe.

Interest Rate: Record the interest rate for each debt. This is crucial as it will help you prioritize which debts to tackle first.

Minimum Monthly Payment: Write down the minimum amount you are required to pay each month for each debt.

Due Date: Note the due date for each debt. This will ensure you never miss a payment and incur late fees.

Example:
Let's say you have the following debts:

Credit Card A: Outstanding Balance - $5,000, Interest Rate - 18%, Minimum Monthly Payment - $100, Due Date - 15th of each month.
Auto Loan: Outstanding Balance - $15,000, Interest Rate - 6%, Minimum Monthly Payment - $300, Due Date - 25th of each month.
Student Loan: Outstanding Balance - $20,000, Interest Rate - 4.5%, Minimum Monthly Payment - $200, Due Date - 10th of each month.
Step 2: Assess Your Monthly Budget

Now that you have a clear picture of your debts, it's time to evaluate your monthly budget. Look at your income and expenses to determine how much money you can allocate towards debt repayment each month.

Be realistic about your budget and identify areas

where you can cut back on non-essential expenses to free up more funds for debt payoff.

Example:
Suppose your monthly income is $4,000, and your essential expenses (rent, utilities, groceries, etc.) total $2,500. After accounting for these expenses, you have $1,500 left for debt repayment and other discretionary spending.

Step 3: Identify Your Debt Payoff Strategy

Next, choose a debt repayment strategy that aligns with your financial goals and preferences. Two popular methods are the Snowball Method and the Avalanche Method.

Snowball Method: With this approach, you focus on paying off the debt with the smallest balance first, while making minimum payments on other debts. Once the smallest debt is paid off, you move on to the next smallest debt. This method provides quick wins and builds momentum as you eliminate debts one by one.

Avalanche Method: In this method, you prioritize paying off the debt with the highest interest rate first, while making minimum payments on other debts. By tackling high-interest debts first, you minimize the total interest you'll pay over time and potentially pay off debts faster.

Example:
Let's say you choose the Snowball Method. You will focus on paying off Credit Card A first, as it has the smallest outstanding balance.

Step 4: Allocate Your Monthly Debt Repayment Funds

Now, it's time to allocate your available monthly debt repayment funds among your debts based on your chosen strategy. Take the extra funds you identified in your budget assessment and distribute them towards your debts.

Example:
With $1,500 available for debt repayment each month, you decide to allocate $300 to Credit Card A (minimum payment + additional funds), $300 to the Auto Loan (minimum payment + additional funds), and $400 to the Student Loan (minimum payment + additional funds).

Step 5: Set Up a Debt Payoff Timeline

Establish a realistic timeline for paying off each debt, considering factors like interest rates and the amount allocated towards each debt. Use a debt payoff calculator to estimate how long it will take to become debt-free based on your current strategy.

Example:

Based on your debt payoff plan, the estimated timeline is as follows:

- Credit Card A: Pay off in 18 months
- Auto Loan: Pay off in 50 months
- Student Loan: Pay off in 54 months

Step 6: Monitor Your Progress

Regularly track your debt payoff progress and make adjustments as needed to stay on course. Celebrate each debt milestone you achieve and stay motivated throughout the journey to debt freedom.

Example:

After six months of disciplined payments, you notice that you have paid off $1,800 of Credit Card A, reducing the outstanding balance to $3,200. You're on track to becoming debt-free!

Developing your debt payoff plan is a significant step towards achieving a debt-free retirement.

By evaluating your debts, choosing the right strategy, and creating a realistic timeline, you'll gain control over your finances and work towards a more secure future.

Remember to connect this exercise to the broader context of retirement planning, where managing debts plays a crucial role in building a solid financial foundation for your golden years.

Stay committed to your plan, stay disciplined, and enjoy the peace of mind that comes with knowing you're actively working towards financial freedom. Your debt-free retirement awaits!

Chapter 10

Planning for Healthcare Costs Ensuring a Healthy Retirement

Taking proactive steps to address your healthcare needs will grant you peace of mind and allow you to savor the golden years with confidence.

In this chapter, we will explore the intricacies of healthcare planning for retirees , providing you with step-by-step guidance and realistic examples to navigate this important topic effectively.

Understanding Healthcare Expenses

As you reach your retirement years, one of the first steps to ensure a healthy future is to understand the range of healthcare expenses you may encounter.

Healthcare costs can include medical insurance premiums, deductibles, copayments, prescription drugs, and long-term care expenses.

Let's explore each of these in detail:

1. Medical Insurance Premiums: These are regular payments you make to maintain your health insurance coverage.

You may have different options, such as Medicare Part B premiums, Medicare Advantage plan premiums, or private health insurance premiums if you choose to keep private coverage.

2. Deductibles and Copayments: These are out-of-pocket costs you incur when you receive medical services. Deductibles refer to the amount you need to pay before your insurance kicks in, while copayments are fixed amounts you pay for each visit or service.

3. Prescription Drugs: As you age, you might require medications for various health conditions. Understanding your prescription drug coverage and potential out-of-pocket expenses will be essential for budgeting your healthcare costs.

4. Long-Term Care Expenses: Long-term care encompasses services needed for daily living activities if you become unable to care for yourself independently. These services could include assistance with bathing, dressing, eating, and mobility. Long-term care costs can be significant, and planning ahead is crucial.

Medicare and Other Healthcare Programs

As you plan for healthcare costs, one of the key components is understanding Medicare. You become eligible for Medicare at age 65, and it offers different parts to cover various aspects of healthcare:

Medicare Part A: Covers inpatient hospital care, skilled nursing facility care, hospice care, and some home health care.

Medicare Part B: Covers outpatient services, doctor visits, medical supplies, and preventive care.

Medicare Part C (Medicare Advantage): Private insurance plans that provide Part A and Part B benefits and may offer additional coverage, such as prescription drugs or vision care.

Medicare Part D: Covers prescription drugs and can be obtained as a standalone plan or as part of a Medicare Advantage plan.

Understanding the different parts of Medicare, enrollment periods, and potential costs will help you make informed decisions about your healthcare coverage.

Additionally, you should also explore other healthcare programs available for retirees, such as Medicaid and supplemental insurance (Medigap), to supplement your coverage and potentially reduce out-of-pocket expenses.

Evaluating Your Health Needs

A critical step in planning for healthcare costs is evaluating your health needs.

Assessing your current health status, considering any pre-existing conditions, family medical history, and lifestyle choices will provide valuable insights into the level of healthcare coverage you may require in the future.

For example, if you have a chronic condition that requires ongoing treatment, you may want to choose a health insurance plan that provides comprehensive coverage for your specific needs.

Budgeting for Healthcare

Creating a dedicated healthcare budget within your overall retirement financial plan is essential to ensure you can manage potential healthcare expenses without compromising your financial security.

Let's break down the process of budgeting for healthcare costs:

1. Identify Your Fixed Healthcare Costs: These are regular expenses that you can anticipate, such as insurance premiums and prescription medications.

2. Account for Variable Healthcare Costs: These are expenses that may fluctuate based on your health needs, such as copayments for doctor visits or unexpected medical treatments.

3. Anticipate Long-Term Care Expenses: Considering potential long-term care costs in your budget is critical. Long-term care insurance, if appropriate for your situation, can be a valuable addition to your healthcare plan.

Factor in Inflation: Healthcare costs tend to rise with inflation, so it's essential to account for this when creating your budget.

By diligently budgeting for healthcare costs, you can ensure that you are financially prepared to handle your medical needs during retirement, granting you the freedom to focus on enjoying your golden years.

Health Savings Accounts (HSAs)

One valuable tool to consider for saving and investing for future healthcare needs is a Health Savings Account (HSA). HSAs are available to those with a High-Deductible Health Plan (HDHP), and they offer triple tax advantages:

Contributions to an HSA are tax-deductible, reducing your taxable income in the current year.

The money in your HSA grows tax-free, allowing your investments to potentially grow over time. Withdrawals from an HSA for qualified medical expenses are tax-free, providing you with tax-free healthcare funds.

Contributing to an HSA can be an excellent strategy to save for future healthcare costs while enjoying valuable tax benefits.

Long-Term Care Planning

As you plan for retirement, it is essential to consider long-term care needs. Long-term care services can be expensive, and addressing this aspect of healthcare early on can protect your assets and give you greater control over your care choices.

There are several options for long-term care planning, including:

1. Long-Term Care Insurance: A dedicated long-term care insurance policy can provide coverage for assisted living, nursing home care, and home care services. The earlier you secure this insurance, the more cost-effective it can be.

2. Self-Funding: Some individuals choose to self-fund their long-term care needs, relying on their savings and investments. This approach requires careful financial planning and budgeting for potential long-term care expenses.

3. Hybrid Long-Term Care and Life Insurance Policies: These policies combine long-term care benefits with life insurance, providing a death benefit to beneficiaries if long-term care benefits are not used.

By exploring and evaluating these options, you can make an informed decision about long-term care planning that aligns with your needs and financial capabilities.

Preventive Care and Wellness

An essential aspect of healthcare planning is prioritizing preventive care and wellness.

Regular preventive screenings, vaccinations, and healthy lifestyle choices can play a significant role in promoting a healthy retirement.

Incorporate these preventive measures into your healthcare plan to reduce potential healthcare costs and ensure a higher quality of life.

End-of-Life Care and Estate Planning

While sensitive, planning for end-of-life care is an essential consideration in healthcare planning.

Having a living will, healthcare directives, and a comprehensive estate plan can provide peace of mind and ensure that your healthcare wishes are respected if you are unable to make decisions for yourself.

Estate planning also helps protect your loved ones and ensures that your assets are distributed according to your wishes.

Evaluating Insurance Options

As you plan for healthcare costs during retirement, it's essential to evaluate various insurance options to find the most suitable coverage for your needs..

For example:

Medicare Advantage Plans: These plans are offered by private insurance companies and provide the same coverage as Original Medicare (Part A and Part B) while often including additional benefits, such as prescription drug coverage or dental and vision care.

Medicare Prescription Drug Plans (Part D): If you choose Original Medicare, you may want to consider adding a Part D plan to cover prescription medications.

Medigap (Medicare Supplement) Policies: Medigap policies help fill the gaps in coverage that Original Medicare doesn't cover, such as copayments, coinsurance, and deductibles.

Medicare Advantage and Part D Plans Change Yearly: Remember to review and compare your plan's changes each year during the annual open enrollment period to ensure it still meets your healthcare needs.

By carefully evaluating these insurance options, you can find the coverage that best fits your needs and budget.

Seeking Professional Advice

Navigating healthcare planning during retirement can be complex, so seeking advice from qualified financial advisors and healthcare professionals is crucial.

Financial advisors can help you create a comprehensive healthcare budget and integrate healthcare planning into your overall retirement plan.

Healthcare professionals can offer valuable insights into your health needs and potential future healthcare requirements.

In conclusion, planning for healthcare costs during retirement is a significant aspect of ensuring a healthy and secure future.

By taking a proactive approach and making informed decisions, you can create a comprehensive healthcare plan that aligns with your unique needs and financial goals.

Remember to explore the intricacies of Medicare, consider long-term care options, and invest in preventive care and wellness.

CHAPTER 11

Addressing Common Retirement Concerns

As retirement approaches, it's natural to have questions and uncertainties about what lies ahead.

I mean, this is a big transition, and it's completely normal to feel a mix of excitement and apprehension.

But fear not! In this chapter, we're going to tackle those worries and give you the confidence you need to navigate this new chapter in life.

Common Fears and Worries About Retirement

You might be asking yourself, "Will my savings be enough to cover all my expenses?" or "What if unexpected healthcare costs arise?"

These are valid questions, and we've got your back! Remember our discussions in Chapter 6 about diversifying your investments and creating a balanced portfolio?

This will ensure your money continues to work for you during retirement, easing financial worries.

Another way to conquer retirement anxiety is by staying mentally engaged. Consider exploring part-time work or volunteer opportunities that align with your interests and skills.

This will not only provide a sense of purpose but also supplement your retirement income.

In Chapter 10, we explored Considering Part-Time Work or Retirement Delay, and now we can dig deeper into the process of exploring various part-time opportunities that resonate with you. Imagine how fulfilling it would be to continue doing something you love while enjoying the perks of retirement!

Tips for Coping with Uncertainties

Uncertainties are a part of life, and retirement is no exception.

But here's the good news: you can develop strategies to cope with these uncertainties effectively.

One useful tip is to create a budget and track your expenses. This will give you a clear picture of your financial situation and help you make informed decisions. In Chapter 4, we covered Creating a Realistic Savings Plan, and budgeting was a crucial part of that process.

By knowing where your money is going, you'll feel more in control of your financial future.

Additionally, consider diversifying your income streams. This can be achieved through a combination of retirement accounts, investment income, and potentially part-time work.

Diversification reduces your reliance on a single source of income and provides a safety net against market fluctuations.

We touched on diversification in Chapter 6, and now we can delve deeper into its significance in managing retirement uncertainties. After all, having multiple streams of income can give you peace of mind knowing you have more financial security.

Ultimately, remember that you are the architect of your retirement journey.

By leveraging the knowledge and insights we've gathered throughout this book, you can confidently navigate the common concerns and uncertainties associated with retirement.

The key is to plan wisely, stay informed, and remain adaptable to life's twists and turns.

So, embrace this phase of life with an open heart and a curious spirit. Retirement is a new chapter filled with opportunities to explore, grow, and enjoy the fruits of your labor.

Take a deep breath, know that you are well-prepared, and let's tackle those retirement concerns together! Remember, you've got this, and we're cheering you on every step of the way. Happy retirement planning!

CONCLUSION

Congratulations on completing this transformative journey towards a fulfilling retirement! Throughout this book, we've explored every aspect of retirement planning, from envisioning your ideal retirement to building a robust financial strategy.

We've dug deep into understanding investment options, addressing common concerns, and providing actionable advice to ensure your retirement dreams become a reality.

As you close the final chapter of this book, remember that retirement planning is not merely a destination but an ongoing adventure.

Your life is a tapestry of experiences, and retirement is a new canvas upon which to paint your dreams.

By taking charge of your financial future and embracing the knowledge you've gained, you have the power to craft the retirement you've always envisioned.

This journey has been about empowering you with practical tools and actionable insights, but it is also about celebrating the unique journey you're embarking upon.

Your retirement is a time to cherish the memories you've made and embrace the possibilities that lie ahead.

From setting SMART goals to diversifying investments, from creating a flexible budget to staying committed to your financial journey, each step has brought you closer to the retirement you desire.

Remember that life is dynamic, and your plans may evolve, but with the solid foundation laid by your thoughtful preparations, you're well-equipped to navigate through any twists and turns.

While financial stability is crucial, let's not forget that the heart of your retirement lies in the experiences, relationships, and joy you'll encounter.

Whether it's pursuing long-lost passions, spending quality time with loved ones, or exploring new horizons, your retirement is a canvas awaiting your brushstrokes.

As you venture into this new chapter of life, remember that you are never alone.

Seek guidance from professionals, involve your family, and share your dreams with friends who have also embarked on this journey.

Together, you can build a supportive network that enriches your retirement experience.

Lastly, let us extend our heartfelt gratitude for choosing this book as your guide. Your dedication to securing your financial future and embracing a fulfilling retirement is commendable.

As you face the challenges and joys ahead, carry the wisdom from these pages and let it empower you to make confident decisions.

Your retirement journey is unique and personal, and the possibilities are as vast as your imagination. Embrace it with open arms, celebrate every milestone, and savor the moments that make life truly extraordinary.

As the author of this book, I leave you with my warmest wishes for a prosperous and joyous retirement. May your days be filled with laughter, love, and adventures that enrich your soul and leave a lasting legacy for generations to come.

Cheers to your magnificent retirement journey and I wish you a remarkable retirement and a life well lived.